LONDON SARTORIAL

First published in the United States of America in 2017 by
Rizzoli International Publications, Inc.
300 Park Avenue South
New York, NY 10010
www.rizzoliusa.com

Design and Art Direction
Paul Solomons and David Hicks

Picture editors
Anna Akopyan and Cai Lunn

Contributing photographers

Jonathan Daniel Pryce
Terence Donovan
Simon Webb
Rhys Frampton
Mike Blackett
Dylan Don
Thomas Cooksey
Daniel Riera
Scott Trindle
Sean Thomas
Rebecca Thomas
Mark Kean

Contributing Stylists

Luke Day
Jo Levin
Victoria Higgs
Gary Armstrong

ISBN: 978-0-8478-5866-8
Library of Congress Catalog Control Number: 2016958771

2017 2018 2019 2020 / 10 9 8 7 6 5 4 3 2 1

Printed in China

Page 4: Terence Donovan. Advertisement for Terylene, London 1960
Page 5: London Collections Men SS17 show, June, 2016

LONDON SARTORIAL

MEN'S STYLE

FROM STREET TO BESPOKE

DYLAN JONES

RIZZOLI
NEW YORK

New York · Paris · London · Milan

CONTENTS

INTRODUCTION

LONDON IS
THE HOME OF MENSWEAR

BY DYLAN JONES

I

t was a Wednesday some time late in the afternoon in November, 1996. The phone rang in my office, put through by an intern on the front desk. On the other end was a rather flustered journalist from *Vanity Fair*, obviously in need of some help: "Yeah, er, hi there. We're doing this London special and wondered whether you could suggest some people to photograph. We're sending some of our guys over in a few weeks and this London thing is a little difficult to pin down."

Isn't it always. Hapless correspondents from the likes of *Time* and *Newsweek* have always found that it's simply not enough to wander the streets of Camden or Chelsea, attend a few fashion shows and force your way into the odd nightclub or two to find the current version of Swinging London. In 1996, Europe's sexiest city was as difficult to pin down as it ever is, and the spirit of the age back then was just as likely to be found in a swanky loft development in Clerkenwell or a tumbledown drinking club in Notting Hill as it was in Knightsbridge or Soho.

The really interesting thing about London at the moment, however, is the activity in the high street, or rather, just behind it. Forget for a minute the gargantuan designer stores opening along Bond Street and focus instead on the independent boutiques that have emerged in Shoreditch, Marylebone and Soho, the eclectic little stores that can now be found in Columbia Road, Lambs Conduit Street or Duke Street. London has always been full of stylish boutiques, but these days there are so many places that are not only drop-dead, cutting-edge hip, but are also part of a long-standing tradition of independent London menswear retailers whose raison d'etre is a highly particular style, loosely called "modernist dandy."

You can call them hipsters if you like, but they've always been here.

This sartorial prototype can be traced back all the way to the Sixties, when men in numbers were just

beginning to display the same self-regard that many more men do today. In the tradition of the London aesthetic, the style they shared was amorphous, an inherited style which first flourished in the independent boutiques in the King's Road and Carnaby Street. What they had in common was a passion for clothes and a shared vision, as well as a common antecedent.

In a way many of the people involved in London's current menswear boom can be traced back to Austin's, the famous Shaftesbury Avenue store which stocked Arrow and Brooks Brothers button-down shirts as well as many other staples of mock-Americana. Austin's was where the now-legendary London retailer John Simons bought his first American button-down, a move which eventually caused him and his partner, Jeff Kwintner, to open The Ivy Shop in 1965, perhaps the most influential men's clothes shop in post-war Britain.

Situated on Richmond Hill in south London, it became an oasis of East Coast American cool in a city fixated by the showy glamour of Carnaby Street, a home-from-home for all those surrogate modernists who fancied themselves as the next Anthony Perkins, Cary Grant, Gerry Mulligan or Bob Newhart. Like many of their contemporaries, Kwintner and the lugubrious Simons were obsessed with the Ivy League, and The Ivy Shop was the first place in the UK to import Madras button-down shirts, penny loafers, Levi's straight-leg chinos and wing tips, the heavy black brogues favoured by USAF lieutenants.

It was an almost pathological obsession. "He cared about more than profit," wrote Nik Cohn of Kwintner in his celebrated 1971 history of post-war menswear, *Today There Are No Gentlemen.* "When he started to talk about his business, he alternated great reams of theory and schemes with flashes of distrust. 'Why should I reveal my innermost thoughts to you?' he said. 'You're only dabbling, you're not involved: how could you understand?' For these reasons, I found him intriguing and likeable. He had flashes

of true fanaticism." Cohn went on to call Kwintner the most influential pop shopkeeper since John Stephen, the man who helped invent Carnaby Street.

"Our aim was to sell the best American clothing in Britain," says Simons. "Carnaby Street was happening at the time, but we appealed mainly to young guys whom we used to call modernists, which is what we were. I think that The Ivy Shop definitely had a hand in defining mods. There was a Carnaby mood before us, but we appealed to people who were sharper. We were terribly self-conscious."

"The Ivy's shoes really did it for me," says David Rosen, a long-time observer of the scene, whose estate agency is one of the few non-tailoring outlets in Savile Row. "Wing-tips, cordovans, smooths, tongue and tassel loafers, penny loafers—they sold just about everything: Harrington jackets, Sta-Press, Brooks Brothers, the whole kit. They defined modernism."

Simons and Kwintner's success with The Ivy led them to open a second outlet, The Squire Shop, in Brewer Street in 1969, and then a third, The Village Gate, two years later. Having changed the way that many British men bought their clothes, as well as inventing the Harrington jacket (so-called because it was a variation of the golf jacket worn by the character Ryan O'Neal played in Peyton Place, Rodney Harrington), Simons moved out of the business for the best part of the Seventies, opening another preppy haven, John Simons, in Covent Garden in 1981.

In the past thirty years The Ivy's legacy has continued to grow like a family tree, with many of the more interesting London shops able to trace themselves back to those post-war days of austerity and rationing. Both Stuart Molloy and Philip Start were Saturday boys at The Ivy before going on to start their own businesses (Jones and Woodhouse respectively), for instance, while Peter Siddell, who owns The Library, used to work for Molloy.

Ashley Lloyd-Jennings of Hackett used to work with Molloy, while Jennings and his partner, Jeremy Hackett, both used to work for Browns, as did the Savile Row tailor Richard James. Kilgour's Carlo Brandelli was once embroiled in The Duffer of St George (which has its own roots in Jones). And so it goes on.

To a certain extent, all these shops were fashioned from the ashes of The Ivy, albeit in contrasting ways: Hackett produce clothes for dandified gentlemen, Richard James specialises in made-to-measure, while Jones, Browns and The Library excelled at directional, high-priced designer wear; The Duffer of St George, Woodhouse and The Squire Shop all produced own-label collections, aimed at every type of modern hipster. Sharp, classic clothes for sharp, classic men.

"The Ivy was a remarkable place because it really created a new mood in London," said Stuart Molloy, owner of the long-gone Jones, one of the few shops in Covent Garden's Floral Street which didn't belong to Paul Smith. "Not only was it selling the type of clothes which you couldn't buy in Britain, but it also attracted the kind of people who were obsessed with the modern world. It created an atmosphere where people were encouraged to go out and do their own things. I worked at The Squire Shop with [society photographer] Richard Young and, knowing that he liked photography, Jeff Kwintner bought him a camera and encouraged him to start taking pictures. That's how Richard Young became a paparazzo [in media circles he is now nearly as celebrated as the stars he photographs]. It's quite astonishing to look around London and see all these people and shops which are connected in some way with that period. Most of us are doing very different things, but we all shared the same interests, the same spirit."

Fashion is the most postmodern of all arts, unable to reinvent itself without acknowledging the past. In days gone by this was often seen as an occupational hazard, an unavoidable curse, though now it is a prerequisite to look at any decade through the rose-tinted spectacles of the twenty-first century. By 1996 this modern aesthetic could be found in restaurants (Oliver Peyton's Coast), hairdressers (Peter Smith, the barber of Savile Row), jewellers (Solange Azagury-Partridge) and furniture shops (Tom Tom in New Compton Street). Everywhere from the home of the exquisite—Connolly, in Knightsbridge—to the home of the bizarre—Vent, in Ledbury Road.

The lingua franca of this stark indulgence (la dolce avenger, the new dandyism, call it what you will) soon became well defined: shops with interiors which looked like sets from *The Umbrellas of Cherbourg* or Jacques Tati's *Playtime*. Places full of Arne Jacobsen Egg chairs, Tom Dixon lights, geometric arc-lamps from Le Paul Bert, Tom Tom or Succession, an Eames chair, the books of Jane and Michael Stern and maybe the occasional etching by the likes of Bridget Riley, Richard Hamilton or Eduardo Paolozzi. Places where you were attended to by the shorn-haired assistants dressed in Timothy Everest, John Pearse or Ozwald Boateng, spruce spread-collar guys overburdened with charm and attitude. Richard James was certainly a spread-collar, double-cuff kind of guy, a maverick designer whose exquisite suits, shirts and ties made him popular with everyone from Liam Gallagher to Terence Conran.

"We design unfashionable clothes, and by that I mean classics, modern English classics. We are anti-fashion in a way," said James at the time. "Traditions are different these days. You don't go grouse shooting, you buy it from Sainsbury's. Consequently, a huntsman's jacket now has different connotations. We wanted to open a tailors which wasn't buried in the past."

These days, fashion for men in London has an echoic force. Seriously, has the male Londoner ever looked as good as he does today? It's unlikely. Not as many people were watching him back then, of course, back before men became as objectified as women, but you get my drift. Cast your eye around town: men have a swagger about them today, a licence to flaunt, and a real sense of self. Today, all the style tribes, perhaps for the first time ever, are all seriously on fleek.

In the digital agencies of Old Street, formerly the home of dishevelled creatives, you'll now find a gentleman that magazine features desks insist on referring to as the "urbane lumberjack." He hasn't shed the hipster codes—

Above: John Stephen, tailor,
Carnaby Street, London, February 1964

Below: John Stephen Clothes Shop,
Carnaby Street, London, 1967

note the beard and the hiking boots—but those hiking boots are upscale Red Wings, his beard is expensively oiled and he has dressed the whole thing up with a seriously loud windowpane-check woollen suit. Genius! Well, maybe not genius, but clever, thought out. Different.

Or head down to the King's Road, from which the Sloane Ranger had seemingly not budged since Peter York first noticed him way back when (Chelsea is now like those parts of North America that are completely proscriptive in the way they expect men to dress—even the Russians and the French who move here are wearing yellow corduroy trousers and unironic Gucci loafers within two months of arrival), and you'll find the eminently sprezzier "nu-Sloane." This chap is still at home in a coral-coloured shirt and expensive ill-fitting jeans, but rather than imitating his father he has rejuvenated the get-up with man-jewellery (a Tateossian bracelet perhaps, or a Stephen Webster skull ring, the sort that tells anyone who's interested that you're a little bit rock'n'roll, but not too much—like a temporary tattoo, I suppose), an Aztec belt, possibly a hat—and he's swapped the deck shoes for a limited-edition pair of quilted Chuck Taylor Converse.

Even men who like to kick about in tracksuits and trainers are suddenly looking sharp. Not all of them, mind, not the ones you see walking the Holloway Road with white bull terriers on blue baling twine, but the professionals who wince at the thought of wearing a Savile Row suit to work. Whereas a penchant for wearing sportswear outside the gym was once a social death sentence (custodial, no remand), you can now go to Soho House and feel positively out of touch if you're not wearing "sports luxe." Quick recap in case you've been living under cobblestones: this is the style popularised by the likes of Kanye West and comprises couture sneakers (high tops and excessive colours preferable) designer sweatpants (if they cost anything less than a week's salary, they don't actually count) and a smattering of more formal items. You'll see it among retired hedgies as much as the fashion crowd. The office where I work is particularly fond of a version of sports luxe that was once spotted in Mayfair: loose grey jogging bottoms, a black T-shirt, and a blazer made from fleece accessorised with a pocket square. Take that, Kanye.

In the same way that our cities are full of mingled architectural styles—Victorian warehouses, Georgian terraces, twentieth century suburban dwellings, twenty-first century upended vitrines—they're also full of extraordinarily varied street styles. Diverse as they may be, all these tribes have one thing in common: they spring primarily out of an interest in style rather than music. Unlike punks, goths, or ravers, members of this current wave prioritises luxury, quality, and craft. That's why one type we keep seeing, the "modish rocker" is actually a complete misnomer. His Chelsea boots, skinny jeans and leather jacket—probably with a tight-fitting shirt unbuttoned to the sternum—are a direct reference to bands like The Clash and The Libertines, but actually he's got far less interest in Joe Strummer or Carl Barât than he does in Louis Vuitton and Yves Saint Laurent. In many ways, high fashion is no longer a signifier of pop culture—in Britain it *is* pop culture. Look at all those Instagram images of men showing off their sockless brogues or selvedge denim turn-ups. The #menswear tag may attract derision in some quarters but it captures a swell of popular interest in dressing well, and doing so for its own sake. Long may it last.

There is an abundance of virtuoso demonstrations of what can be achieved sartorially when the curiosity and will of the dandy dovetails with the force of the market. If you want to mix a neon neoprene superhero cape with a pair of scarlet matador-inspired short-shorts paired with a skin-tight string vest and floral-patterned knee socks, you'll not only be able to find your items in a flash via your computer—or in a mad taxi dash around the West End, you'll also be photographed by someone immediately—could be for *i-D*, could be for *Mr. Porter*, *GQ*, even Scott Schuman—aka The Sartorialist, and the man who claims to have invented fashion street photography.

Menswear in London has never been more exciting, nor more comprehensive, and there has never been so much of it. Men these days expect great clothes at every price level, be that high street, mid market, designer, luxury or bespoke. They expect quality at any price, and this is something that London delivers. Whether you are shopping in Bond Street or Shoreditch, whether you are taking your credit card down Lamb's Conduit Street or so Mount Street, or flitting between Regents Street and the King's Road, in London there is something for every man.

London is the home of menswear. We invented the suit, and in Savile Row we have the most important men's shopping street in the world. While the Row has always appealed to the establishment, in the last two decades it has opened itself up so much, that it now attracts customers from all four corners. From Gieves & Hawkes at one end, to Richard James at the other, from Anderson & Sheppard round the corner, to Patrick Grant's Norton & Sons, these days the Row offers not just the best in traditional suiting, but the very best in contemporary formal wear.

The city is also full of haute streetwear, or what some have called "luxury ladwear." This new look eschews tailoring and eccentricity and plays to the gallery on the street.

"For the past few seasons, there has been a growing divide between two clear camps: peacock and hyper-casual," said Morwenna Ferrier in *The Guardian* not so long ago. "One is effeminate, an imaginative take on the Brummellian dandy; think leopard print at Topman Design or printed shirts at Burberry. The other is streetwear and its various sub-styles—tracksuits, longline sweaters and textured hoodies. It's a look Danish designer [Astrid] Andersen has made her trademark for the past four seasons. But only now is it coming out on top, as London Collections Men has demonstrated."

Ferrier called this "smart lad," and she is not wrong.

"It is casual but I don't call it casualwear," said Andersen. "That just boxes it in. I mix the [jogging] bottoms with a longer formal jacket, so it's both formal and casual. It can be both."

This new boom in British menswear is something I tried to reflect when, at the behest of the British Fashion Council, I helped set up London's first men's fashion week, London Collections Men (as it was then called) at the end of 2011. Typically, the idea of a fashion week dedicated especially to men started as a desire to compete on the global stage with the likes of Paris, Milan, and New York, the other major cities that have held similar weeks for decades.

For what seemed like years, the menswear element of London Fashion Week was always tacked on to the end of the women's shows, almost as an afterthought. But there had increasingly been so much interest from designers wanting to show, and so much interest from the press and consumers alike, that it was decided by the British Fashion Council to create our own men's fashion week, and to move it to a more relevant time in the calendar. After all, by the time of the men's day at the end

of LFW, all the important press and buyers had disappeared to Milan in order to see the Gucci show, and—far more importantly—the day was in completely the wrong part of the season.

Which is why we moved it so that our men's fashion week now precedes those of Florence, Milan, Paris, and New York. The British Fashion Council asked me to chair the initiative, and so along with the BFC's CEO Caroline Rush, I spent six months not just espousing the idea, but trying to encourage those British designers who had previously decided to move abroad—Burberry, Alexander McQueen, Vivienne Westwood, etc.—to move back and show in London.

We knew that in order to encourage all the press and buyers to put another three days in their diaries and come to London, we had to make the experience fun. We wanted them to wake up in Milan (the fashion week that immediately follows ours) with the mother of collective hangovers. We wanted them all to tell anyone who would listen: "You know what? I went to London and I had a seriously great time."

Our pitch to designers was simple: come and show your clothes in the coolest capital in the world, come and show your wares in the city with the best restaurants, the best museums, the best art galleries, public spaces, parks, hotels, and cocktail bars.

Come where the action is.

Sure, you could choose to show your clothes in Milan. But then you'd be showing your clothes in the ugliest city in northern Europe that isn't in Germany. Sure, you could show your clothes in Paris. But then you'd be showing your clothes in the most bourgeois city in Europe. Alternatively, you could choose to show in New York. But then you'd only be showing in the most neurotic city in the world.

Seriously, why would you want to be anywhere other than London?

We were also aware of needing to celebrate our wonderful city. These days London is less a metropolis and more of a lifestyle choice, a place from which to launch yourself into the world, or a place to land having investigated everywhere else (and obviously found them wanting). The latest iteration of Swinging London is a wonder, with a multitude of reinvigorated urban villages, new art galleries and more A-list restaurants per square mile than any other city in the world. So in a way, LCM became as much of an advertisement for

London as it is for our burgeoning (as well as established) menswear talent.

We asked Prince Charles to officially launch LCM for us, and convinced Elton John and David Furnish to throw open their home for a dinner and a showcase by the hot new band The Strypes. We asked magazines and newspapers to get involved and have parties (the project wasn't going to work unless it was inclusive, and everyone felt as though they could take ownership of it), and we asked celebrities to become ambassadors, encouraging them to spread the message on television and radio (our ambassadors initially included the hip-hop star Tinie Tempah, broadcaster Nick Grimshaw, model David Gandy and TV behemoth Dermot O'Leary—they were soon joined by Formula 1 racing champion Lewis Hamilton, Chinese supermodel Hu Bing and film producer and philanthropist David Furnish himself).

After a few seasons, the mayor's office began to see the commercial possibilities of LCM, especially in terms of attracting visitors to London. In his capacity as the Mayor of London, Boris Johnson stepped up to the plate (what suits does he wear? Everyone from Marks & Spencer to Hugo Boss), as did the mayor's head of cultural policy, Justine Simons, encouraging us to work with UKTI, Visit Britain, the Museum of London, the V&A, and even the GREAT Britain campaign to build various cultural and retail programmes. Commercially London is already seeing the benefit of increased revenue for ancillary services such as hairdressers, models, make-up artists, production companies, digital providers, hotels, taxis, restaurants, public relations agencies, and media.

The total global media value generated by London Collections: Men in its second season exceeded £40 million, which is no small beer, even for a week that is largely driven by champagne. Market research group Mintel says the UK menswear market itself has grown by twelve per cent in the past five years and is currently worth £10.4 billion. The group believes the market will maintain this growth and will have risen by eleven per cent by the end of 2016. The direct value of the UK fashion industry to the UK economy is £21 billion, while fashion's wider contribution to the economy in influencing spending in other industries is estimated to stand at over £37 billion.

We have also had a few surprises. One of the things we had not anticipated was the overseas interest in heritage, which is something we tend to ignore in this country. The press and buyers from Asia and the Americas were especially keen to attend our Savile Row events and loved being able to visit St. James's Palace, Jermyn Street, Spencer House, St. Paul's, Lord's Cricket Ground, and all the other cathedrals of tradition where we held events. Because of this, we asked then-prime minister David Cameron to host a press reception for the fashion industry at Downing Street, which is not the sort of thing that would happen anywhere else in the world (can you imagine the US President launching New York fashion week at the White House, or François Hollande inviting Karl Lagerfeld to the Élysée Palace?).

Predictably, the other fashion capitals were not exactly thrilled by what we were attempting to do. Some of the senior figures at our rival organisations went public with their disdain for the idea, some made a great point of ignoring us, while other lobbied hard behind our backs, trying to convince their designers to stay put. However, one of the great by-products of setting up a men's fashion week in London is the fact that we have attracted international fashion designers from everywhere—from New York, Beijing, and Paris to Milan, Copenhagen, and Hong Kong.

"I am very pleased to be showing my menswear collection in London," said Tom Ford, who we encouraged to move to London from Milan. "London has a vibrancy that is inspiring and much of what I create for men takes its inspiration from traditional British menswear. My clothes are designed with an international customer in mind, and London is one of the most international cities on the planet."

London Collections Men came about because we felt that menswear was suddenly becoming more interesting than womenswear. For the first time in an age, British menswear felt as though it had the Big Mo, felt as though it had some serious traction.

There are now more commercially minded, critically acclaimed young menswear designers than ever before, people such as Agi & Sam, Jonathan Saunders, Lou Dalton, JW Anderson, Craig Green, and Matthew Miller. Unlike the menswear designers with whom I grew up in the Eighties, and who filled the pages of style magazines like *i-D*, *The Face* and *Blitz*, this new generation understand that in order to compete on a global stage, you need a properly commercial business, not just a bunch of press cuttings from trendy Japanese magazines.

London has obviously been a centre of subcultural excellence since the early Sixties, when the likes of David Bailey, Michael Caine, and Mary Quant redefined the city as a template for the future. Since then, every decade, usually around the mid-point, London has risen up again: punk, club culture, Britpop, you name it, London has been the centre of it.

And menswear has always been at the heart of this cultural rebellion. Not only do we have the greatest tailors in the world in Savile Row, not only do we have the best youth culture and street style in the world (we invented everything from the Teddy Boy to the punk), we also have some of the world's most high profile fashion designers in Paul Smith, Christopher Bailey, and the Alexander McQueen brand.

The potential of menswear is exponential. There is a feeling even among those who stand to lose the most by such an admission that womenswear has almost reached a state of saturation, and that while the fashion industry continues to spread around the globe, it is in menswear where the real innovation is happening. The men's market has traditionally been a lot smaller than the women's market, but as the women's business slows, so the men's business expands. This of course has been due to one thing and one thing only: consumer demand. Men these days expect great clothes at every price level, be that high street, mid market, designer, luxury or bespoke. They expect quality at any price, and so far the market appears to be delivering it. The current generation of male consumers might be more sophisticated than previous generations, and they might not shop more like women, but because of that they no longer have any qualms about buying into the idea of "fashion." Men these days treat clothes almost as a fait accompli. There is no stigma attached to them, nothing secret.

And London is at the centre of it all. "London is the creative heart of the Burberry brand and has such a unique energy," says Burberry's Christopher Bailey. "Steeped in the incredibly rich tradition of British menswear but with outstanding, innovative young talent coming out of its design schools. I'm so inspired by that mix of heritage and modernity, along with a few iconic Brits that I admire who are references for the show. I think British style is much more about a mindset than a 'formula.' For me, its charm lies in its effortlessness —a sort of thrown-together elegance, coupled with a quiet confidence."

This quiet confidence is something that can be found among many of the designers showing at London Collections Men, a confidence that appears to be growing season by season, just as it appears to be growing in pretty much every postcode in town. It is a confidence reflected on the catwalks, too, as London is also the only fashion capital that genuinely reflects racial diversity.

Now, as far as menswear is concerned, we have form. And if anyone ever asks you just why Britain is so good at menswear, and so good at producing menswear designers, then you only need to say this: not only are the British good at tradition, we excel at rebellion too. Britain, and especially London, is awash with great sartorial heritage, both recent and historical. Not only do we have the greatest tailors in the world in Savile Row—we did, lest we forget, invent the double-breasted suit—we are also responsible for every major youth cult since the end of the Second World War: everyone from Edwardians, Teds, mods, hippies, skinheads, punks, and New Romantics were all born on the streets of London.

At its best, fashion has always been about play-acting, a way of artificially presenting one's self to the world, an elaborate form of disguise or fancy dress. Fashion still has the ability to shock us in ways to which we think we've become immune, and over the years it has encouraged us to look like gypsies, tramps and thieves, as well as hoodlums, members of the Baader-Meinhof gang or undernourished Nepalese peasants.

To the world at large, London really became the centre of street style during the Swinging Sixties. Looking back now, it almost seems as though everything happened at once. In a decade dominated by youth, London burst into bloom. It was swinging, and it was the scene. The Union Jack suddenly became as ubiquitous as the black cab or the red Routemaster, and all became icons of the city. Carnaby Street's turnover was more than £5 million in 1966 alone (money absorbed from the West End's own "Carnabetian army," in Ray Davies's famous words). Quite simply, London was where it was at. In the space of a few months the skies over London had become kaleidoscopic, full of multi-coloured swirls and curls, and curlicues of every imaginable shape and size. It was as though colour had replaced coin as a symbol of wealth and success, as though pigment were the cure for all known evils. There appeared to be no affliction not tempered by the application of some glitter mascara, or the donning of some extravagant garb. Colour became almost confrontational. Fuelled by growing prosperity, social mobility, post-war optimism and wave after wave of youthful enterprise, the city captured the imagination of the world media. Here was the centre of the sexual revolution—the pill had been introduced in 1961—the musical revolution, the sartorial revolution. London was a veritable cauldron of benign revolt.

And so it is today.

Menswear is something we are extraordinarily good at. It is an intrinsic part of British heritage and history.

Just look at the three-piece suit: Even more so than the double-breasted suit (or, as we've always called it in the GQ office, the double-barrelled suit), the three-piece suit is the most intimidating form of formal daywear. And it was invented in Britain, first adopted by Charles II and then described by Samuel Pepys as "a long Cassocke close to the body, of black cloth, and pinked with white silk under it, and a coat over it, and the legs ruffled with black riband like a pigeon's leg."

The three-piece was a business staple during the Eighties, when it was sported by a generation of young bankers who wanted to dress as well as act the part. Most wore boxy off-the-peg numbers, although those who really knew what they were doing had theirs made, sometimes by a Savile Row tailor, but often by "a little man I know in the East End."

One of the fundamental mistakes that a man can make when buying a three-piece-suit is not making sure that the waistcoat fully covers the top of the trousers. This is especially important if the person commissioning the suit is of the corpulent variety.

Modern practitioners of the suit include Giorgio Armani, Zegna, Tom Ford, and Richard James, although all Savile Row tailors have noticed a return to the three-piece. For years the three-piece gave way to the two-piece, as customers opted for a more casual type of dressing, but recently, as an antidote to the effect of dress-down Friday, those who care about such things have been wearing more and more three-pieces. As the *Wall Street Journal* said not so long ago, "The three-piece suit has been asserting itself with increasing frequency on designer runways, as well in the collections of traditionalists. They're now a fixture of men's fashion magazine spreads. And they're popping up more in pop culture, on celebs including Bradley Cooper and Usher, and on TV characters such as Roger Sterling of *Mad Men* and Patrick Jane (played by Simon Baker) on *The Mentalist*. They're even showing up on gangsters in HBO's period show *Boardwalk Empire*."

And no one does it better than a Savile Row tailor.

There is no street more important to the world of menswear than Savile Row. It is here where international menswear designers come when they want to understand the principles of the bespoke suit, here where the international traveller comes when they want to buy the very best tailoring that money can buy.

There is simply no other street like it, nowhere in the world that is so dedicated to men's clothes. The Row is also more inclusive, more welcoming and more egalitarian than it has ever been. In previous times, the Row was where you went if you were entering "society," if you were an English gentleman, a man of the cloth or a man of letters. The middle and working classes were only encouraged to visit if they were tradesmen, cutters or chauffeurs. The English class system was one of the strictest in the civilised world, and its manifestation was obvious in Mayfair, not least in Savile Row.

These days, however, the street has welcomes the world with beautifully turned pinstripe arms, enveloping a new domestic and international customer. Times have changed, the world has moved on, and Savile Row has finally woken up to the fact that collectively it is one of the most influential fashion hubs in the entire industry.

A decade ago, should you have wandered the Row in search of some retail therapy, and should you have entered the portals of one of the street's legendary bespoke tailors, you may have been met by an octogenarian gatekeeper who would have sized you up the second you opened your mouth. The cutting rooms would have been quiet, and the process of choosing your suit (the cloth, the cut, the style) would have been fairly proscriptive.

Now, though, these rooms are alive with activity, with a new generation of tailor, a new generation of customer, and a sense that far from being part of London's long established heritage industry, Savile Row is—dare we say it?—hip.

As well as this great heritage and diversity, these days, we also have some of the world's most high profile fashion designers in Paul Smith, Christopher Bailey and the Alexander McQueen brand. We have Alfred Dunhill, Church's, DAKS, Edward Green, Gieves & Hawkes, Hackett, Henry Poole, Richard James, Mulberry, Oliver Sweeney, Thomas Pink, and more. And while some of these brands might be owned by foreign conglomerates, it is British craftsmanship that keeps them at the very forefront of the industry.

One of the latest games to tickle the fancy of the average Londoner is Spot the Tie. So few men wear ties to work these days that it's almost become a sartorial anachronism. Men these days are smarter than ever, investing in all kinds of formal suitings; yet they seem increasingly reluctant to wear a tie. Dress-down Friday has

a lot to answer for, and one of the manifestations of this short-lived gimmick (men coming to work in their pyjamas, or looking as though they were just about to clean the car or walk the dog) was the confinement of the necktie to the bottom drawer.

Which means that wearing a tie is now one of the easiest ways to make a statement. It is even considered to be power dressing. Especially if you use a Windsor Knot.

The Windsor is one of those hoary old things you find in arcane gentleman's guides, and tying one is still considered to be one of those things a man of breeding should be able to do with his eyes closed. Every man ought to, and it is actually incredibly easy to master (almost as easy as the four-in-hand, the one you used to use every day). All you need is a little bit of practice.

The knot is so-called because it was meant to be the brainchild of the Prince of Wales, later King Edward VIII, and later still the Duke of Windsor (the exportable dandy) when he abdicated. There is now evidence that his father, George V actually wore what became known as the Windsor, although his son certainly appeared to popularise it (preferring to wear his ties with a spread collar, which is still the best way to show one off). You can actually achieve the same effect as a Windsor by using the four-in-hand on a very thick tie, and there is now proof that this is actually what the Duke did himself. Lord Lichfield, the current Queen's cousin, photographed the Duke tying his tie in a four-in-hand in the Sixties in an effort to dispel the myth, but to no avail.

Whatever. A man wears a Windsor because it makes the knot look fat, and looks particularly impressive when worn with a double-barreled hipster suit. Especially if you're a "modernist dandy."

And those dandies appear to be everywhere. Just look at the success of GQ. Twenty-five years ago we had to appeal to that select band of aspirational men who wanted to look good; now, every man wants to look good.

However, not every man wants to be told how to go about it. As someone who has spent the last quarter of a century attempting to do that, I know how carefully one needs to tread. Perhaps it's still safe to assume that men might need a little more help than women when it comes to looking good, but we are a lot less keen on admitting it.

And one thing we're not keen on at all is being told someone is a style icon. In womenswear, the term "style icon" is pervasive almost to the point of cliché. From Jane

LONDON
COLLECTIONS:
MEN

Birkin and Audrey Hepburn to Kendall Jenner and Alexa Chung, these women wield considerable influence over how other women dress and, sometimes, what designers choose to show each season.

With men it's slightly trickier, because we like to think we know how to dress without being overly influenced by anyone else. Consequently, calling someone a "style icon" is tempting fate.

However, there are various qualities that a man needs to have not only to qualify as a bona fide style icon, but to be accepted by other men as one. First, you need to look effortlessly cool, as though you haven't tried too hard. This is why we still revere men such as Steve McQueen and Hunter S. Thompson, men who were revered for their chosen careers as well as the cavalier ways in which they dressed (often just jeans and T-shirts).

Conversely it helps if you are a true sartorial maverick, someone like David Bowie—not that there is anyone remotely like David Bowie, God rest his soul—who always went against the grain, and genuinely led fashion as opposed to following it or interpreting it.

Then again you have one-offs like David Beckham, an everyman who has spent the best part of his post-football career turning himself into a successful brand and doing it in a way that appeals to men who may not have liked him when he was a Manchester United player.

When we thought about who appoint as ambassadors of London Collections Men (which has now slowly been rebranded as London Fashion Week Men's), we actively sought out popular figures who represent a wide variety of disciplines, as well as a wide variety of demographics.

Frankly we have been lucky that all our ambassadors agreed to get involved with LCM, but then they are all a natural fit, not only because they are all famous, but each and every one of them has a keen fashion sense, and an ability to articulate that to a wide audience.

So in that sense they are all genuine style icons, all men who resonate with the Great British male.

And we are extremely glad to have them.

So these days I think it's fair to say that while there will always be style icons from the past who continue to influence us—and here we could mention everyone from Cary Grant and Paul Weller to George Best and Jarvis Cocker—the style icons who have real cut-through with the modern British man are contemporary figures.

Which obviously means that David Bowie—a true menswear talisman—is still a style icon, something he's been for the last fifty years, something he will be forever.

Dylan Jones

From top left:

Hu Bing, LCM ambassador at the Dunhill cocktail event, June 2016, London

Lulu Kennedy, London, 2013

Tinie Tempah and Lewis Hamilton at the LCM Opening Reception, June 2015, London

Singer and actor David Bowie is photographed for Interview magazine on October 8, 1994 in Los Angeles, California.

Dylan Jones and the LCM ambassadors at the Opening Event, January, 2015, London

Lucky Blue Smith, Eric Underwood, Jack Fox, Josh Ludlow, David Furnish, Tommy Hilfiger, Johannes Huebl, Oliver Cheshire, Robert Konjic, Jack Guinness, and Paul Sculfor attend a dinner hosted by Tommy Hilfiger and Dylan Jones to celebrate The London Collections Men AW16 at Mortons on January 10, 2016 in London, England.

MST

YLE

HU BING

ACTOR, MODEL

Shirt "This Shanghai Tang shirt one of my favourites. I like the traditional Chinese black frog buttons. It's 100 per cent cotton so it's really comfortable and it can be dressed up or down." shanghaitang.com

Shoes "I really like the material transition of this Jimmy Choo loafer; from white suede to black leather. It's bold yet sophisticated. And I really like the contrasting tassels—the left shoe has black and red, while the right one is black and blue." jimmychoo.com

Watch "I love the craftsmanship, uncompromising detail, and modern aesthetics of this Piaget watch. It also has to be one of the thinnest watches I own, coming in at 3.65millimetres thick." piaget.com

SEAN FRANK

ARTIST, FILMMAKER

T-shirt "Uniqlo is my go-to for basics, like this white T-shirt. They always seem to keep on-trend while offering classic, uncomplicated alternatives." uniqlo.co.uk

Suit "I've worn this Paul Smith suit to various events, such as Nick Grimshaw's birthday party. But once I wore it at Christmas, which was a bit of an error." paulsmith.co.uk

Brogues "I really like these Carven shoes because they take the classic shape of a brogue, but have dots all over the shoe. They use the same material that high visibility cycling gear is made from." carven.com

MANRUTT WONCKAEWO

DANCER, CREATIVE DIRECTOR

Hat "I wear a hat because my hair's always a mess. I like wearing inflatable crowns and toys as fashion accessories." achildofthejago.com

Shoes "I always choose colourful shoes. I'm lucky to have size seven feet, so I can fit into both women's and men's shoes." viviennewestwood.com

Jumper "I get lots of my jumpers and T-shirts from Jonathan Saunders. He uses interesting colour clashes." jonathan-saunders.com

Necklace "All my necklaces are from Bitsch Kitsch, Saharat Eddy's stall on Brick Lane. I even have a pair of plastic false teeth as a necklace." backyardmarket.co.uk

Suit "Most of my suits are from Paul Smith; I love his use of colour and print. I also have suits of his in electric blue, peach and turquoise." paulsmith.co.uk

ADIO MERCHANT

SINGER, SONGWRITER

Sunglasses "I feel round frames are the ones right now. These Toy Shades suit my face much better and they have that hippie trippy motion. That's a good thing." toyshades.com

Jacket "This leopard jacket is a bit louder than my usual style. The print is current but they've tried to make it slightly different with really small love-hearts. It's in the detail." youmustcreate.com

Tunic "Let's not use 'man dress' to describe this Lost & Found top. It's got that Arabic cut, especially at the bottom – I feel like it's one of those things that is creeping into fashion. It's beautiful." lostandfoundrooms.com

Shoes "I've got a few pairs of Dr Martens for festivals because they're so big, robust and easy to clean. And they're still a stylish shoe—with the right cut pants they always look pretty amazing." drmartens.com

SAMM HENSHAW

SINGER, SONGWRITER

Hat "I always wear hats because I hate worrying about my hair. A cap paired with a baggy T-shirt creates a scruffy skater look that I really like." baileyhats.com

Jacket "I like the military look. It looks cool tied around the waist. I also love bold jackets inspired by *The Fresh Prince of Bel-Air*." vans.co.uk

Trousers "I'd never worn chinos until I was given these on a shoot. I usually go for a slouchy style, but I thought they looked amazing." topman.com

Watch "I'm not a connoisseur, but I like the brown leather look. And I haven't taken my handmade purple bracelet off in five years." fossil.com

Socks "I love quirky socks and showing them off. These from Topman are simple, but I wore bright blue ones with pineapples on tour." topman.com

Shoes "These Kickers were a Christmas present to myself. I have over forty pairs of shoes, which makes my mum angry!" kickers.co.uk

JACK GUINNESS

MODEL, DJ

Beard "Murdock London barbershops are great for a little trim. My beard grows incredibly fast—Irish genes, no doubt." murdocklondon.com

Silk scarf "Second World War fighter pilots complained to their girlfriends about their heavy jacket zips irritating them. Scraps of silk were used to protect their chests." joshuakanebespoke.com

Sunglasses "These are Toms' James Honey Tortoise sunglasses. Every pair you buy helps pay for someone in the developing world to have their sight restored." toms.co.uk

Suit "This is my Joshua Kane Brummell oversize-black-and-white-check three-piece suit. Kane is an emerging tailor with a distinctive aesthetic." joshuakanebespoke.com

JIM CHAPMAN

VLOGGER, MODEL

Jumper "For this time of year, a turtleneck jumper is everything you need. I like this Reiss one—it's well-fitted and sits beautifully on me." reiss.com

Coat "I got this Burberry coat in New York. I proposed to my fiancée earlier that week, and she bought me this. Burberry is where I go when I treat myself to luxury." burberry.com

Trousers "These Burberry trousers were a Christmas present from my fiancée. She chose well! I tend to mix and match them with a suit." burberry.com

Boots "These Russell & Bromley boots are easy to wear. They're wide around the ankle and wear well under trousers and jeans." russellandbromley.co.uk

BAYODE ODUWOLE

CREATIVE DIRECTOR

Hat "The hat is a Pokit ridge-top Panama. I wear it a lot in the summer." pokit.co.uk

Bow tie "The bow tie is upscaling. I got it from a leftover box of chocolates. That's the Pokit attitude to clothing. It's cool, it's rugged, but you can't take it too seriously."

Teddy bear "I had the bear made by Grin & Bear in honour of my son being born. It's a finger up to that *Brideshead Revisited* look we've churned out, so it's a bit of a witticism." grinandbear.net

Suit "This is my everyday suit. There's a modesty to it where the silhouette says everything: it's short, boxy, and relaxed." pokit.co.uk

AMAN SINGH

ARCHITECT, MUSIC PRODUCER

T-Shirt "I picked this up in a thrift shop in the US. It came in one of those bulk bags of clothes where you get two kilos for a few dollars. This was a hidden gem."

Trousers "I wear these trousers all the time. They're so easy to dress up, but I can also wear them with trainers." christopherkane.com

Watch "It's a limited edition; Bulgari did a series of 500 pieces named after cities. It's definitely the one I save for special occasions." bulgari.com

Trainers "The sole glows in the dark, so these are great when you go on a night out. It's nice to have some funky trainers in your wardrobe." size.co.uk

JAMES BAY

SINGER, SONGWRITER

Hat "I found this hat in Nashville while I was making my album. It's an Akubra hat, which is an Australian brand. They were selling them in this amazing shop called hatWRKS; their collection is insane." hatwrks.com

Shirt "This shirt was from the Burberry show. It's in a mini-corduroy material. Burberry have this classic, timeless thing going on, which I really gravitate to." burberry.com

Jacket "Last September, I played Christopher Bailey's Burberry show at London Fashion Week. I was able to go and pick some stuff out, and I saw this leather jacket. It felt right and I got to keep it." burberry.com

Jeans These are a classic pair of Topman jeans. I can't go wrong with them—I've been buying Topman stuff since I was fourteen. I like skinny jeans. They have a rock 'n' roll nature to them." topman.com

Boots "These are Clarks Original Desert Boots. They're in ebony vintage. I've been wearing various pairs of these boots on stage for about three years. They get more interesting over time." clarks.co.uk

JASON ATHERTON

CHEF

Shirt "I get my shirts from Smyth & Gibson. You can wash and press them over and over again and they still look brand new." smythandgibson.com

Suit "I've bought a few things from Thom Sweeney. I feel their suits hit the right balance of not being too trendy or old-fashioned." thomsweeney.co.uk

Shoes "Berluti shoes are very well-made, and beautifully hand-stitched. They also have great after-service." berluti.com

JONATHAN DANIEL PRYCE

PHOTOGRAPHER

Hat "I nearly always have a hat on. At fashion week people always see me with a hat on, so when I don't wear one, people don't recognize me and walk straight past me. I used to wear a trilby or a fedora, but now I'm a photographer I need to wear very practical hats."

Jacket "I like it because it's thin like a shirt but it is a jacket. And it's slightly waterproof because it's got a coating on it. I tend to like wearing a denim jacket under an overcoat in winter." levis.com

Watch "I love Shinola's story. It's the champion of a new workforce in Detroit after the city went bankrupt." shinola.co.uk

Jeans "They are probably the only jeans I ever wear because they're proper selvedge denim and they fit me so well: wide and a straight leg all the way down."

Shoes "These Converse are wider than standard Converse, with a thicker sole, an insole on the inside and stronger canvas. I have a few pairs of these—when I see something I like I get a lot of it." converse.com

TONY WARD

MODEL, FASHION DESIGNER

Polo top "When looking for the perfect linen shirt, go with someone you trust. Depending on the occasion, I'll roll the sleeves up and keep the top buttons undone to add a dressed-down twist." jigsaw-online.com

Suit "I'm a fan of waistcoat suits like this Jigsaw two-piece. I love the ones that I've collected over the years—they make me feel as though I've made an effort." jigsaw-online.com

Watch "Rolex is the daddy of watch brands and this Air-King model is all about quality and longevity." rolex.com

Holdall "I take this Ede & Ravenscroft holdall with me when I go travelling. I usually carry a book, fedora, and something beginning with an *i*—iPad, iPhone, etc.—to keep in touch with the world." edeandravenscroft.com

Glasses "I love geek chic like these Gucci glasses. It's a move away from my usual look, so it surprises people." gucci.com

Shoes "I like that these Oliver Spencer Tracker shoes are a modern twist on a classic. How many shoes do I own? Ask my wife; I share a shoe closet with her." oliverspencer.co.uk

JAMES NUTTAL

FASHION DIGITAL MARKETING GURU

Hat "I go cycling with my friends all the time—I ordered some team caps from Walz, and they sent an extra set of free ones, too. This colour matches my jacket." alwaysriding.co.uk

Jacket "This is a classic bomber. I've worked with Jonathan Saunders, and this was part of a private order I put in. People say how good he is with colour, and I think that's true." matchesfashion.com

Trousers "With basics like these CP Company trousers, it's all about the fit. These are tapered to the ankle, but they're not too tight." cpcompany.co.uk

Shoes "Converse shoes go with everything. These are a special edition from the Seventies collection; they look just that bit better than a normal pair. They're such a classic." office.co.uk

LOCATION LOCATION LOCATION

PHOTOGRAPHY JONATHAN DANIEL PRYCE

PARK

LIFE

PHOTOGRAPHY JONATHAN DANIEL PRYCE

The
KIDS
are
ALRIGHT

PHOTOGRAPHY MARK KEAN AND REBECCA THOMAS

STYLING, GARY ARMSTRONG AND VICTORIA HIGGS. MODEL: NICK RUMP AT SELECT, MATT DORAN AT PRM, JACK BURKE AT D1 MODELS, ALEX BLAMIRE AT FM LONDON, FINNLAY AT ELITE, ZIGGY VON THUN-HOHENSTEIN AT MILK, NED BARTON AT ESTABLISHED MODELS.

LONDON

CALLING

PHOTOGRAPHY JONATHAN DANIEL PRYCE

PINSTRIPE PUNKS

CITY OF LONDON

PHOTOGRAPHY THOMAS COOKSEY
STYLING LUKE DAY

EC1

HAIR STYLIST. BEN JONES AT JED ROOT. **MAKE UP.** ELIAS HOVE AT JED ROOT.
MODELS. RHYS PICKERING AT BANANAS MODELS. MATS AT NEXT. HANNES GOBEYN AT MODELS BY KEEN.

Photo assistants Jim Agnew, Guillaume Blondiau, Jori Komulainen and Harry Burner. Stylist's assistants Sophie Clark and Ben Schofield. Production Katy Offley Productions.

LIKE
A
ROLLING
STONE

PHOTOGRAPHY SEAN THOMAS
STYLING JO LEVIN

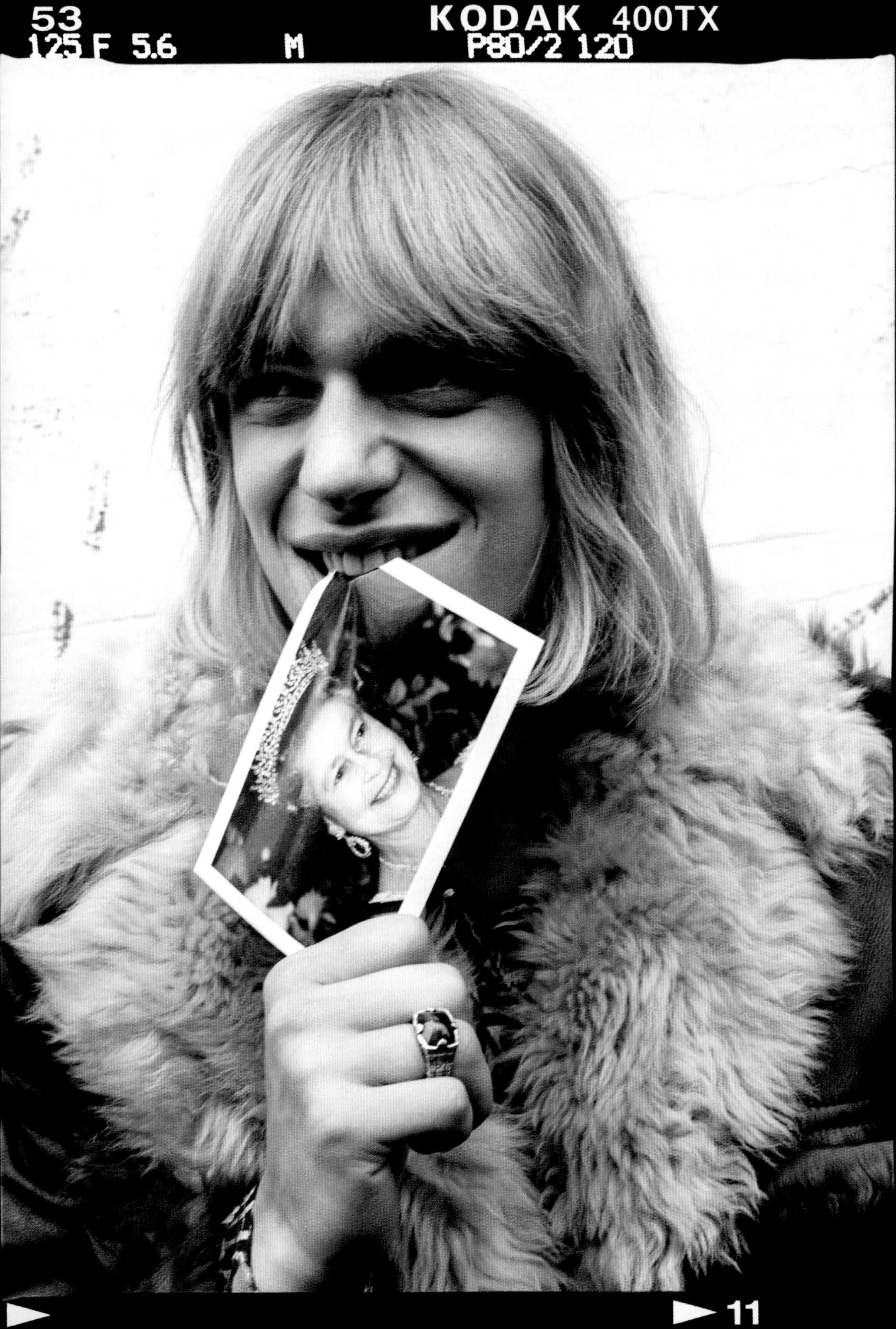
53
KODAK 400TX
125 F 5.6
M
P80/2 120
11

►1

HAIR & MAKE UP. GARY GILL FOR EMOTIVE MODEL. TON HEUKELS AT MODELS 1.

Hair Stylist's assistant Holly Roberts Production Grace Gilfeather

WEST END

BOYS

PHOTOGRAPHY DYLAN DON

STYLING JO LEVIN

TAKING

CARE

OF

BUSINESS

PHOTOGRAPHY DANIEL RIERA

STYLING LUKE DAY

BRIT

PHOTOGRAPHY SCOTT TRINDLE   STYLING LUKE DAY

POP

HAIR STYLIST. CHI WONG AT JULIAN WATSON AGENCY. MAKE UP. NAOKO SCINTU AT SAINT LUKE ARTISTS.
MODELS. SIMON FITSKIE AND MIHAI BRAN AT ELITE, ALFONS MIARI AT SUPA,
LIAM GARDNER AT SELECT AND CALLUM WARD AT PREMIER.

Photo Assistants Fabian Nordstrom, Simon Mackinlay and Philip White. Hair stylist's assistant Montana Lowery. Stylist's assistants Sophie
Clark and Ben Schofield. Digital technician Neil Pemberton. Production Katy Offley Productions. Casting director Shelley Durkan.

DESIGNER PROFILES

AGI & SAM

AGAPE MDUMULLA & SAM COTTON. FOUNDERS

Agape "Agi" Mdumulla and Sam Cotton, otherwise known as Agi & Sam, have shown at every season of London Collections: Men since it started in 2012—and every time they've received a standing ovation from the notoriously tough crowd. Their USP? Coming up with inventive, game-changing prints inspired by their travels, whether that be a jaunt on London's public transport or a trip to Tanzania. London is part of their DNA, and they are much sought-after barometers of modern British street style. They have partnered with big brands such as Topman and UGG, won *GQ*'s Breakthrough Fashion Designers Award in 2014, and the following year won the first-ever British regional round of the International Woolmark Prize. Their appeal lies not just in their consistent idiosyncrasies, but also in their personalities, which shine through their clothes likes golden thread. They know exactly who they are and exactly what they're doing. And the world is a much better place because of it. They are also blessed with a great sense of humour: in January 2015 they sent their models down the catwalk with their faces covered in Lego. At the time, Mdumulla said, perhaps with his tongue in at least one of his cheeks, "We wanted to enjoy what we are doing, make fun and playful clothing, and here it's almost as if the wearer can build their own clothing." It won't surprise anyone to learn that Agi actually started designing at the age of four.

ALEXANDER McQUEEN

SARAH BURTON, OBE, CREATIVE DIRECTOR

Stepping into Alexander "Lee" McQueen's boots was never going to be easy, but then replacing an iconic fashion designer is always a problematic professional transition. The succession however has been even more successful than anyone could have envisaged. Having worked with McQueen for fourteen years, Sarah Burton carefully tweaked the house's aesthetic, whilst always being mindful of McQueen's legacy (and, more importantly, of the enhanced legacy she knew he was going to slowly acquire). "At the beginning I just wanted to keep his legacy intact, to keep telling the stories," she says. "I thought I'd be capable of finishing his stories, but I didn't know if I could tell my own." As it transpired she actually had more than she needed. Taking the McQueen menswear show from Milan to London was also a bold move, although a perfectly fitting one for such a resolutely British brand.

SS.15

141

ASTRID ANDERSEN

FOUNDER

Astrid Andersen always gives you a punch to the stomach, creating premium casualwear with a sports-inspired aesthetic that aims to jump-start the next generation of menswear. This is sportsluxe with knobs on. She is a Danish-born designer who graduated from the MA fashion menswear course at the Royal College of Art in 2010. Her graduate collection was styled by one of the very best fashion editors in the world, Simon Foxton. "The person who listens to A$AP Rocky is interested in what I represent, so they buy my clothes," she says. "At the moment menswear just has greater excitement [than womenswear], and that comes from the guys on the street changing everybody's perception. As a designer, I'm just translating that. I do find my biggest inspiration from guys in the street. They have all the power."

CALM AND SUNNY,
BUT THE AIR IS FULL OF BULLSHIT

86

This London-based design duo were both 2010 graduates of the London College of Fashion. United in their belief that, in spite of living in an increasingly rapacious industry, beautiful craftsmanship and imaginative design make for sustainable principles, Wouter Baartmans and Amber Siegel have fostered a directional premium label focusing on wearable luxury. Their London Collections: Men presentations are styled by the Fashion Director of *Esquire*, Catherine Hayward, and have become something of a must-see, not least for their innovative staging. Baartmans and Siegel are also not worried about being too literal. For instance, their fall 2016 collection was heavily influenced by the clothes worn in Seventies underground clubs up in Manhattan's Spanish Harlem, their details and shapes reflecting the eccentric style of characters who looked as if they were paying a lot of attention to contemporary cinema. Some standout looks from this collection included a reversible bomber that had leopard-print rabbit fur on the inside and black neoprene on the outside, and two amorous cockerels rendered in beautifully intricate embroidery. Another bomber came in a gigantic dogtooth jacquard with embroidered snakes crawling on its back. This was more than a nod to Scorsese's *Casino*—this was an homage to loungecore pimp, a whirl through the avenues and alleyways of old-skool New York.

BAARTMANS
and SIEGEL

WOUTER BAARTMANS & AMBER SIEGEL, FOUNDERS

Founded in 1924 by Eli Belovitch and his son-in-law Harry Grosberg in Staffordshire, for years Belstaff was renowned for making all-weather jackets for motorcyclists. The Belstaff biker's jacket quickly became one of the most iconic pieces of traditional British menswear, a jacket that was fashionable because of its purpose, its simplicity, and the fact that it never changed. In 2004, Ewan McGregor and Charley Boorman travelled 19,000 miles from London to New York via Western and Central Europe, Ukraine, Russia, Kazakhstan, Mongolia, Siberia and Canada for the documentary *Long Way Round*; both men wore Belstaff jackets. Like most British companies initially associated with particular products, Belstaff has expanded its range and now offers collections that cater to men and women who have probably never been on a parked motorbike, let alone a moving one. After a brief spell in Milan, Belstaff moved back to London, keen to associate themselves once more with a home-grown market. The brand's menswear Creative Collection Director is Delphine Ninous: "LCM is very important to Belstaff as we are a British brand and showcasing new collections in London is key in communicating this. The Belstaff pionerring spirit fits in with the energy and creativity of London designers."

BELSTAFF

DELPHINE NINOUS, CREATIVE COLLECTION DIRECTOR

BURBERRY

CHRISTOPHER BAILEY,
CHIEF CREATIVE & CHIEF EXECUTIVE OFFICER

As one of the world's most powerful designers, Burberry's Christopher Bailey has not only been the creative head of the brand for over a decade, but since 2014 has been its chief executive officer. Since he arrived at the company in 2001, the company share price has increased more than 500 per cent. Along with former CEOs Rose Marie Bravo and Angela Ahrendts, Bailey is the man who brought a modern twist to one of the oldest fashion houses in the world while maintaining its heritage. He's also helped launch the careers of models and musicians alike (Cara Delevingne, Edie Campbell, and Roo Panes to name only three), not to mention catapulting the brand into the digital age with innovative campaigns. Make no mistake: while Burberry might be a truly global brand these days, it is British through and through—as iconic as Thomas Heatherwick's red Routemaster bus or the London Eye—and Bailey insists the brand's history is at the heart of everything. "I always take it back to the trench coat. It can be formal and tailored but also rock 'n' roll. Burberry has a strong world of tailoring, but I try to make this feel effortless and a little bit more relaxed. My ambitions are to push boundaries, communicate in new ways and remain innovative. The world is evolving and technology is making us approach life in a different way, so we have to keep an open mind, stay curious and always question ourselves."

CASELY-HAYFORD

JOE CASELY-HAYFORD, OBE & CHARLIE CASELY-HAYFORD, FOUNDERS

The London-based father-and-son design team formed their company in 2009, essentially to convey their vision of London to an international audience. Mixing sportswear with tailoring, and naturally mixing the old with the new, they've created a new sensibility that appeals to many men. They have a big fan base, and their clothes are worn by Michael Fassbender, Robert Downey Jr, James Blake, Dermot O'Leary, Mos Def, Drake, Steven Spielberg, and more. The press tend to like them, too: "The most accomplished debut London Collections: Men will ever see," trumpeted *i-D*. Unsurprisingly, the duo love London, and Londoners. "I come across a lot of people," says Charlie, "and I don't know whether this is just an East London thing, but they work in a number of different disciplines at the same time—'slashies.' It's difficult because I think people automatically assume that it's because you're not very good at one [thing], you decide to do a number of different things. But I think it's quite interesting and it seems to be in East London that you can actually, if you are creative, dip into a number of different things. Even though I do come across a lot of slashies, I don't write them off straight away, because I think that it's a product of out generation's post-modernism."

CHRISTOPHER KANE

FOUNDER

Christopher started his label with his elder sister, Tammy, soon after completing his MA at Central Saint Martins school of art in 1986. Spearheading a revival of British high fashion, the brand soon caught the attention of Kering, which, five years later, announced they were buying a fifty-one per cent share of the company. It was only natural that menswear would soon follow. "Christopher Kane's menswear lives quite comfortably in the shadow of his more prepossessing women's collections," says sagacious menswear writer Tim Blanks, "but it plays a valuable role in that it often renders his current fascinations more direct, especially when the silhouettes of menswear are so familiar. If his collections for men miss the eerie quality that infuses much of his womenswear (when he talks about an influence as unlikely as the cultists of Jonestown, it somehow makes perfect sense in the light of the clothing), they make up for it with an upbeat, boyish accessibility."

Ethical fashion is at the heart of Christopher Raeburn's brand, and when he was showcased in American *Vogue* in 2010 it was under the banner: "Remember the four Rs—reduce, reuse, recycle and Raeburn." One of his earliest signature collections, Remade in England, featured a series of bombers and parkas created from repurposed parachute silk. He describes the typical Raeburn item as being a mix of archaeology and new technology. One of his recent collections made full use of this remade ethos with a bomber jacket and a parka made from a recycled orange inflatable life raft. "Soon you will be able to buy a jacket and when you no longer want it, you can send it back and it will be mulched down into something else," he says. Collaboration is a vital component of his business strategy. He has served both as artistic director of the Swiss Army knife makers Victorinox (perhaps unsurprisingly, his favourite piece from his first project for the label was a cocoon blouson that was made from an old Swiss Army sleeping bag) and produced a remarkable series of products for the Korean backpack behemoth MCM. "The more Raeburn focuses on remade fabrics, the better his collections seem to be," says Suzy Menkes. "The Christopher Raeburn story is one of imagination and perseverance, and, increasingly, well-deserved success. An on-going collaboration with Woolmark and other established brands proves that you can both be good and do good in a fashion world that could use more thoughtful designers like Raeburn."

CHRISTOPHER RAEBURN

FOUNDER

CHRISTOPHER SHANNON

FOUNDER

Christopher Shannon was the first winner of the inaugural BFC/GQ Designer Menswear Fund, supported by Vertu. The Fund was established in September 2013 following in the footsteps of the successful BFC/Vogue Designer Fashion Fund and provides one designer with £150,000 grant to underwrite the infrastructure necessary to take the business to the next stage, as well as £50,000 of in-kind services, including a twleve-month bespoke, high level mentoring support programme. Christopher Raeburn, Christopher Shannon, E. Tautz, Lou Dalton and Richard Nicoll were shortlisted for the 2014 prize and all participated in a mentoring programme where industry experts, including fund committee members Ben Banks and Jonathan Akeroyd, provided guidance on topics such as strategic planning, branding, leadership, commercial retail, e-tail, and wholesale and digital innovation. While the competition was tough, Shannon's win attested to the very bright future of British menswear, demonstrating original flair, meticulous craftsmanship, and in-depth commercial understanding.

COACH

STUART VEVERS, CREATIVE DIRECTOR

Having helped steer luxury brands such as Mulberry, Bottega Veneta, and Loewe, in 2013 Stuart Vevers joined Coach, which entailed his moving immediately from Madrid To New York. "It was definitely a big culture shock," he says. "It is a very different way of working and a very different company. But that was the appeal; I was intrigued having spent most of my career in traditional European luxury. I think my first job was to define what the brand means and what makes it different." As well as being the custodian of the women's line, he was also charged with reinventing Coach menswear, and he did so by launching it in London, at London Collections: Men. Having graduated from the University of Westminster and lived for many years in London, he has a huge fondness for the city, and to him the move made complete sense. "The biggest thing for me was that it took Coach out of context and pushed us to take the collection further. Also, there is a lot of buzz around London and when the management saw the reaction, they told me they were glad I had pushed for it." That first collection was dubbed luxe-without-fuss by the critics and was hailed as little short of a triumph. And to celebrate the city he considers home, the after-party was held at the Lady Ottoline (named after the rather racy woman many critics consider to have inspired Lady Chatterley)—his old local when he lived in Bloomsbury. The food was classic pub fare, too, with Scotch eggs and sausage rolls galore.

CRAIG GREEN

FOUNDER

Craig Green's designs were first shown on-schedule through Topman and Fashion East's MAN show for London Collections Men, while subsequent shows through the initiative have continued to explore a unique marriage between boundary-pushing showmanship and wearability. With the support of NEWGEN Men, Green achieved widespread acclaim with his first solo show, winning a British Fashion Award for Emerging Menswear Designer in 2014. *The Independent*'s Alexander Fury was an early admirer: "[His clothes] are intelligently designed, beautifully executed and created with a minimum of fuss, often utilising humble fabrics like drill and poplin to create maximum impact; an economy that feels invigorating. His voice lends something different to the debate. His work stands out—and in the crowded landscape of modern fashion, that's all-important."

DOLCE & GABBANA

DOMENICO DOLCE & STEFANO GABBANA, FOUNDERS

When Domenico Dolce and Stefano Gabbana decided to support London Collections: Men, it not only validated the event as an international menswear platform, but also injected some vigorous Southern Italian glamour into proceedings. Their first show was spectacular, too, with dozens of beautiful boys in sublime Dolce & Gabbana eveningwear, and Kylie Minogue looking impossibly gorgeous. They produced a party atmosphere that was completely in keeping with the spirit of LCM. When we launched we knew that in order for people to start to put LCM on their calendar that it had to be fun as much as anything else. We were confident buyers and journalists would come and support British creativity, but we wanted to bamboozle them with cocktail parties, dinners, and discos, too. Stefano and Domenico got this from the off, which is why they became honourary ambassadors immediately. "We love London, because London means a good time," they say, collectively. "London is a party."

DSQUARED2

DEAN & DAN CATEN, FOUNDERS

When the Canadian-born design director twins Dean and Dan Catan decided to celebrate their twentieth anniversary as designers they chose Canada House in the heart of London as the venue. After all, they do live in Notting Hill. They were feted by Canadian high commissioner Gordon Campbell, congratulated by the likes of Samuel L. Jackson, Lottie Moss, David Furnish, Jack Guinness, Ellie Goulding, and Ellen von Unwerth, and flanked by a host of male models on the embassy's sweeping staircase. As Bluey Robinson performed, endless glasses of Perrier-Jouët were soaked up by hearty mac 'n' cheese and maple chicken wings. This was high fashion and fast food. The brothers have a simple test when designing for men: "We ask ourselves, 'Would I wear that?' And there's the date test: would I open the door if someone came for dinner wearing that?"

DUNHILL

FABRIZIO CARDINALI, CEO

Ah, the *GQ* office. While we all secretly like to think of ourselves as *Reservoir Dogs*, in our hearts we know we're really little more than reservoir poodles. In our navy blue suits (the ones with the rope shoulders, shawl collars and thin leather piping), our white Dunhill shirts, our skinny ties and ridiculously polished shoes, we act as though we have pistols in our inside pockets, when in reality we probably only have taxi receipts and large Montblanc pens. We'll shoot our cuffs and ostentatiously draw attention to our TAGs, making sure the entire restaurant gets a peek at our Stephen Webster devil cufflinks. Oh, what show-offs we are, attempting to play the part even if we're not always sure what the part is. Bow-wow, woof woof. But although the boys in the office were reservoir poodles long before they were *Mad Men*, I think it's fair to say that the world's finest television programme only made us worse. Dunhill is the perfect brand for anyone who wants to relive the golden age of advertising, whether you consider that particular age to be the Sixties, the Eighties, or, indeed, now. You're certainly going to turn heads—and account, no doubt—walking into a glass lift wearing a midnight blue Dunhill suit and a golden brown pocket square.

E. TAUTZ

PATRICK GRANT, CREATIVE DIRECTOR

In some respects Patrick Grant owns a little piece of Mayfair. In fact, he owns two little pieces, with his flagship premises in Savile Row and a recently opened shop in Duke Street, just off Grosvenor Square. Duke Street is rapidly becoming one of the most important fashion hubs in this part of town, as here, on the northern fringes of Mayfair you'll find an outpost of Jigsaw's Bluebird emporium, the Nick Ashley-fronted Private White V. C., and of course E. Tautz itself, the luxury tailoring brand that Grant relaunched in 2009, as a ready-to-wear label. "Essentially the brand is about clothes that I actually wanted to wear," he says. "I had been working at Norton & Sons, wearing a suit every single day—if you work in a Savile Row bespoke tailor selling suits, it's kind of obvious that you have to wear one. And when I started wearing non-suit stuff because I, say, was in the studio at Tautz, people's eyebrows would raise. E. Tautz clothes are a lot easier to wear and, while sometimes I enjoy the formality of putting myself together in a very structured way, I'm not going to buy my loaf of bread on a Saturday wearing a suit." Grant has also become something of an ambassador for the area, a position helped enormously by his appearance as a judge on the television series, *The Great British Sewing Bee*. He was named the Menswear Designer of the Year at the British Fashion Awards in 2010.

GIEVES & HAWKES

MARK FROST, DESIGN DIRECTOR

These days, anyone can visit a Savile Row tailor, but a century ago it was assumed you had to be of a certain class to get through their doors. If you were the sort of man who went "up west" to get his suit made, you were probably a banker, a politician or a barrister. Or maybe a rock star. You were certainly not just anyone. There is so much rubbish talked about bespoke suits. The only thing you really need to know is that it's incredibly easy to have one made, and that there is no mystery about it whatsoever. Neither is it prohibitively expensive—if you shop around it shouldn't cost much more than an off-the-peg suit from a top-name designer. Savile Row is a far friendlier place than it was fifty, or even twenty-five years ago, and caters to a more modern man: you. There are many things to recommend a bespoke suit. There are the fittings, where you are made to feel like the most important man on Earth (which is a change, perhaps, from how you are treated at home, at the office, or in your local hardware store). There's the knowledge that no one is walking around wearing anything like what you're wearing, and there is the slight decadence of investing in something that many men still find unnecessary. And there's the childish, but still quite satisfying feeling when, having been asked where you bought it, you say your suit is bespoke. Actually. Gieves & Hawkes are one of the most important, one of the most iconic tailors in London, and their rejuvenation under former creative director Jason Basmajian was comprehensive, and completely successful. They continue to slide from strength to strength.

HACKETT

JEREMY HACKETT, CO-FOUNDER

One doesn't tend to think of the Hackett brand as being expert in outerwear. Sure, we consider the label responsible for great British suiting, for fabulous formal shirts and the kind of top-class luxury goods that appeal to the man with both money and taste in his arsenal. Hackett, we think to ourselves, a thoroughly British brand that makes great two and three-piece suits, and which manages to bridge the gap between traditional and contemporary with a knowing smile. Outerwear, though? Have we ever really thought of them as an outerwear brand? We ought to, as in this field—and being in fields is primarily why they're designed—they have form. Come the weekend, instead of tramping up and down Savile Row, Bond Street or Mount Street—peering into ghosted windows and hopping into grey slate restaurants—many Londoners can be found in the manicured backwaters of the Cotswolds, strolling the South Coast beaches, or wandering around the Black Mountains (perhaps carefully putting sheeps' skulls into carrier bags—some people collect them, sheeps' skulls that is, not carrier bags), working up a genuine sweat. These activities demand a different kind of wardrobe, and not one normally associated with the formality of Hackett. But Hackett's outerwear is as good as any you can find in any "weatherwear store." You might think that Hackett produce the kind of protective jackets that would stand up to little but a knowing glance from a disgruntled ex-colleague sitting opposite you in the inner horseshoe in The Wolseley, but actually they can cope with whatever it is the Gods of Weather decided to throw at them. And all this from a company who many probably think was invented in the middle of the City sometime back in the eighteenth century, rather than in a second-hand penguin suit shop in the King's Road in 1980.

HARDY AMIES

DARREN BARROWCLIFF, HEAD OF DESIGN

Back in the Nineties, when the great designer Hardy Amies was still alive, he tried to convince all and sundry of the benefits of the five-button jacket. He was to be respected. After all, this was the man who had dressed the Queen from her accession in 1952 right through to 1989. But no one was quite sure whether this new-fangled idea was going to catch on. However, he was bang on the money elsewhere. Having written a regular column for *Esquire* on men's fashion, in 1964 Amies published the book *ABC of Men's Fashion*. It listed dozens of sartorial commandments, such as this banger: "A man should look as if he has bought his clothes with intelligence, put them on with care and then forgotten all about them." Hardy Amies is a different brand these days, but no less important. Obviously London today is genuinely cosmopolitan in the people and cultures it embraces, and so Amies has moved to accommodate. In terms of men's style, it stresses the interplay between the generations, between town and country, between heritage and technology, between tailoring and casualwear, putting a lot of elbow grease behind the idea that British style for men is more fluid and dynamic now than at any time before. The brand reflects this by making smart, functional menswear that is as at home in Mayfair as it is in Dalston. The look is modern and stylish, without being overtly "designed."

JAMES LONG

FOUNDER

It almost seems as though James Long has been fast-tracked by the industry. He has been supported from the off by NEWGEN, Fashion East, and the British Fashion Council, and, according to *Interview*, "is the unofficial poster child of the London menswear community." At one time, Lanvin's Lucas Ossendrijver even called him his favourite young designer. A mainstay of London Collections: Men, in 2015 Long was also appointed creative director of Iceberg menswear. "As a teenager I used to save up to get the train to Camden with my sister to buy awful clothes," he says, "and we were fascinated with all the people there. I got hooked on London, I got hooked on the fashion. Nowadays I think London is the most interesting place for new talent in menswear in the world, mostly down to the great nurturing that goes on here."

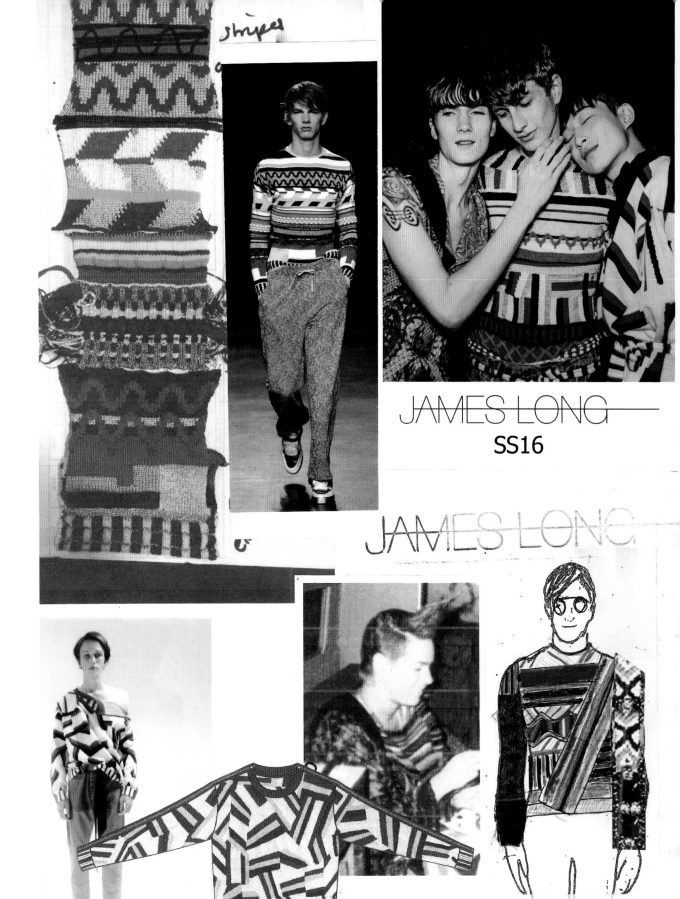

stripes

JAMES LONG
SS16

JAMES LONG

J.W. ANDERSON

JONATHAN ANDERSON, FOUNDER

To say that Jonathan Anderson challenges traditional ideas of menswear is something of an understatement. Some might think he intentionally sets out to shock, but his motivations are far more sophisticated than that. Gender fluidity certainly has a place in his collections, and he is determined the push the metaphorical envelope, but shock value isn't an imperative. As Lou Stoppard said on *SHOWStudio* after his autumn/winter 2016 show, "Anderson put men in lace and frills before anyone else." He says he is a creative director rather than a designer, yet he is one of the very best designers we have. Like Pablo Picasso, he is not above recognising what has come before: when accepting his Womenswear Designer of the Year award at the British Fashion Awards in 2015, just moments after getting the Menswear equivalent, he said, "I want to thank all designers, past, present, and future, which ultimately I get my inspiration from. We live in post-modernist fashion."

KATIE
EARY

FOUNDER

It's not every young British designer who gets to work with Kanye West, but quite rightly Katie Eary—a twenty-first century DayGlo punkette—has taken the opportunity in her stride. He needs her more than she needs him, and while she has partnered with many superbrands, it's her own clothes, her own collections, which mean the most. To her and to us. For instance, her spring/summer 2016 show was all about the notion of youth, and its disturbance. Her My Little Pony prints took the subversion of nostalgia to the "next level" (at least according to *Dazed*), while her fabrics were selected to represent the glossy sheen of childish plastic toys—satins, silks, poly blends—and her prints designed to "overthrow innocence" (which is probably why there were so many giant cocks). "That's the interesting difference between the sexes," she says. "I mean when you're in love, you're in love, but girls just go crazy for boys. Boys are assholes to them and they're just like, 'Hit me again! Push my face across the playground again!' That's hormones for you!" As for her casting: "Polished and beautiful, dirty teenage boys. Beautiful boys who just want to fuck anything that moves."

KENT & CURWEN

DANIEL KEARNS, CREATIVE DIRECTOR

When, in 2015, it was announced that David Beckham had formed a partnership with one of Britain's oldest menswear brands (one that originally made club, college, and regimental ties for Oxford and Cambridge Universities, then immersed itself in the world of cricket), it was obvious they would relaunch the brand in London. As Beckham was going to be involved personally in areas from product development to store design and location as well as creating new collections and fronting marketing campaigns, this would be a big deal. "Kent & Curwen was established in 1926 as a sports-related gentlemen's fashion brand, so it's a perfect fit to have David as a business partner," said Richard Cohen, chief executive of Trinity, at the time.

KILGOUR

CARLO BRANDELLI, CREATIVE DIRECTOR

"At first glance, I admit it can be off-putting," says Stephen Doig from *The Daily Telegraph.* "Clingy, second-skin tops with cylindrical cut-outs around the navel, Lego masks and pink fluffy toys dangling from jumpers with gay abandon—the pictures from London Collections: Men prove the city's most renegade designers don't make it easy for the contemporary man. But aside from catwalk hijinks—the Pepto-Bismol shaded furry suits (that'll be Sibling's last show, all rather joyful and silly) or plastic bags on heads (Christopher Shannon, a comment for I know not what)—LCM serves as a reminder that in the capital's fashion world, we've returned to doing what we do best: men's clothes with clout, substance, and expertise that eclipse other cities." In terms of expertise, you need look no further than the artist and creative director of Savile Row stalwart Kilgour, Carlo Brandelli, who has brought rigorous couture elements to his brand. You can expect to pay a lot for one of his bespoke suits, but then what you're getting is quite unlike anything to be found within the radius of Mayfair. An obsessive, a Modernist, and a didactician to boot, Brandelli has a very particular way of cutting, and a very particular view of how a man should dress.

LATHBRIDGE

PATRICK COX, FOUNDER

In a nutshell this is the vehicle for the return of shoe guru Patrick Cox, who had such huge success in the Nineties with the Wannabe loafer, the shoe that told everyone they could get into the Atlantic Bar & Grill or the Metropolitan with just a wink and a little shoe polish. The shoes became so popular that Cox had to employ a doorman to manage the queues that formed outside his London shop. The shoe worked because it was on message, but also because it didn't scare the horses. "I think the success of the Wannabe loafer is the comfort factor and the cult that built around it," says Cox. "Even if you didn't want to wear them any more because one too many of your friends had them or too many pop stars wore them that week, you'd end up wearing them because they were so comfortable." Having had stints with Charles Jourdan and Cox Cookies & Cake—a food emporium—he's back on his feet. "To be my own boss again is very, very exciting," he says. "I am my own muse, I am size eight, which is sample size, and the justification is really simple: I try on everything and ask mysel, 'Would I wear it?' And if I would, then we put it into production and put it into the collection. But it's great to be back, and London is the window to the world. London is important. All the creativity is here."

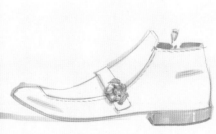

LEE ROACH

FOUNDER

You could call Lee Roach the man who fell to modernism. He left Central Saint Martins in 2010, and in his time has worked with some of the most fastidious designers in the industry, including Meadham Kirchhoff, Carlo Brandelli, and the positively proscriptive Peter Saville. His brand produces clothes that are completely bereft of adornment—"traditional distinctive menswear elements with a new refined minimalism… creating garments that possess sophistication through the process of reduction, eliminating all superfluous components. And he means it. "I'm continually inspired by the principles of reduction and repetition," he says. "I am interested in uniform, modernity, construction, and function, elements that I believe are fundamental to how we dress. Clothes shouldn't wear the man and the man shouldn't wear the clothes. The construction and reduction of the clothes is relevant to modern society where formality and codes of dress have diminished in our daily lives."

LIAM HODGES

FOUNDER

Young Royal College of Art graduate and Fashion East menswear designer Liam Hodges flips traditional luxury upside-down with his hankering for function over flounce. Hodges's collections, which have earned him catwalk sponsorship from the Topman-backed MAN banner and, for spring/summer 2017, from NEWGEN Men, include industrial design techniques, heavy denim and his signature patchwork. They cater to those who live for the week, not just the weekend. The lanky six-foot-six Hodges creates designs that suit those who, like him, need convenient, comfortable clothing: oversized T-shirts, tracksuits, and knitwear. "A sense of the real is what we like," says Liam, "but just a bit better—pushed a little so it's interesting." While functional, Hodges's designs are forward-looking, and they explore mythology, urban folklore, and polysyllabic masculinity. For his first Fashion East installation two years ago, which came about after he was spotted by Fashion East founder Lulu Kennedy at a graduate show, Hodges fused aspects of punk, hip-hop, guerrilla militias (using a load of Gorilla tape), and folk dancing. Hodges wants his brand to be aspirational, but only to an extent. "It's not the archaic idea of aspirational you see in magazines, with £250,000 cars and watches," says Hodges. "We try to build stories of authenticity and passion within our brand that speak to consumers' personalities."

LOU DALTON

FOUNDER

Traditionally Lou Dalton has opened London Collections: Men, an early morning start that always sets a high bar for everything that follows. It's no easy thing kicking off the London menswear shows, but Dalton always does it with aplomb. She launched her label in 2008, having worked for United Arrows in Japan and Iceberg and Stone Island in Italy, where she built upon design skills previously honed during a tailoring apprenticeship. She says that her collections have often been inspired by the men in her life, notably her father and her partner. Coupled with her Shropshire roots (mixed with references to the Apollo space missions, caravan-dwelling farmhands, Texas oil barons, and even Martin Scorsese's *Taxi Driver*), this approach has ensured that Dalton's collections remain grounded in reality. She has produced capsule collections for Dover Street Market, Grenson, Full Circle, Hamish Morow, River Island, Liberty, and Opening Ceremony, and never stops working. Watching her prepare for her LCM shows is an intoxicating experience, as she conjures magic seemingly out of thin air. "London is so inspiring and very welcoming in terms of creativity," she says. "But when I do take time out and have a holiday, the chosen location quite often features in the collection that I'm working on." This once was true of the Shetlands: "I spent almost three years commuting there, all for the love of a man. It's a beautiful, awe-inspiring place to be."

Translated literally from the Sanskrit, Maharishi means "great seer." Founded by Hardy Blechman in 1994, the menswear designer's great vision was to create environmentally sound, fair-trade, long-lasting, utilitarian clothing. Blechman, who previously served in the military, began by producing hemp as well as recycling workwear and military surplus, and Maharishi soon became a cult name on London's streetwear scene. In 2000, Blechman was named Streetwear Designer of the Year by the British Fashion Council, and a year later Blechman launched a second line: MHI. In 2015, Maharishi's autumn/winter collection featured military–style clothing modelled on Japanese ninja costume, which is designed for stealth. The collection included trademark combat trousers, hoods and cross-body bags, and knitwear decorated with Japanese pagoda imagery, and reworked obi belts. The autumn/winter 2016 collection was inspired by garments worn by religious devotees and groups who wear uniform around the world. Maharishi makes frequent use of camouflage, which Blechman, who is now fiercely anti-war, wants to appropriate back to its roots within nature— thereby severing ties to the military. "Combining camouflage prints with reflective materials or using them internally as linings or pocket bags represents a love of camouflage in its representation of nature and art," says Blechman, "and a disdain for it to be used to conceal in order to kill."

MAHARISHI

HARDY BLECHMAN. FOUNDER

MARGARET HOWELL

FOUNDER

If Margaret Howell didn't show twice a year at London Collections: Men it would be easy to think she didn't exist at all. She is the most reclusive of all British fashion designers, even though she is one of the most influential. Her signature designs are the unisex shirt, the gymslip, the lace-up shoe, the duffle coat and the trench coat, but she does so much more. Her beautiful little store in Wigmore Street, just north of Oxford Street in the insanely fashionable Fitzrovia, is an oasis of cool. This retail space sells both her men's and women's collections, accessories, books and furniture. She has also used the shop as a gallery, drawing attention to the likes of Span housing, anglepoise lamps, Robert Welch cutlery, and Ernest Race furniture. In 2007 she was made a royal designer for industry by the Royal Society of Art and was awarded a CBE for services to the fashion industry. In 2010 she was awarded an Honorary Doctorate from the University of the Arts London. No slouch, she.

MATTHEW MILLER

FOUNDER

Matthew Miller has a design philosophy that positions fashion as a product, just like ceramics or furniture, balancing simple manufacturing values with an artist's approach to his craft. Given this, it's not exactly surprising that the visual language of art and gallery spaces is referenced throughout Miller's work, which bears labels reading *Untitled*, *Mixed Media*, *Dimensions Variable* that feature both Ms underscored, a reflection of the choice to call out his initials subtly on a garment rather than plaster his name all over it. He's all about the detail, not about the broadcast, mostly about the micro, less about the macro. Miller sees the wearer as integral to a garment's worth, raising its importance as soon as it's worn because of the cultural capital accrued depending on what he or she does in it—or to it—and so developing the inherent character of each piece. "I never saw beauty as being something that was a physical object," he says, with no hint of embarrassment. "I fundamentally see beauty as being a moment in time, a fleeting feeling, a scar, a memory, an experience, a sense of freedom."

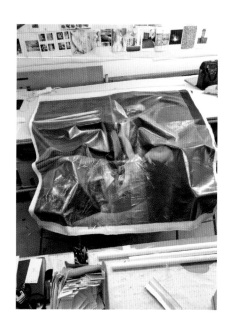

MOSCHINO

JEREMY SCOTT, CREATIVE DIRECTOR

Jeremy Scott's takeover of the legendary Moschino brand has been a complete success, so much so that it's now difficult to imagine anyone else at the helm. In 2015, Scott decided to start hosting his menswear collection at London Collections: Men, and his autumn/winter 2016 show, at a church in Mayfair, was one of the most extravagant in the company's history. In addition to appearances from Lucky Blue Smith, Neneh Cherry, and Jourdan Dunn, it included some collaborative elements from British agitprop artists Gilbert & George. "I wanted to do supersaturated clothes, so I had tea with them," said Scott at the time. "And as I was telling them my ideas for the collection, they said, 'Why don't you take from our archive?' So there were so many wonderful things I was able to incorporate."

MR HARE

MARC HARE, FOUNDER

London has thrown up a whole generation of cobblers, artisans who understand that the first port of call for any status gazers is usually the feet (for the shoes), swiftly followed by the wrist (for the watch). Often, when international buyers want to be into a bit of London without committing to a relationship based on apparel, they buy shoes first, just to see if the kissing's going to work. If it does, then they quickly go to second, third, and home base. Launched in 2009, Marc Hare's shoes are high on quality and craftsmanship. A strong edit of classic shapes is remixed with the brand's trademark vibrancy. Handmade in Tuscany, Hare's shoes are elegant, often colourful, and always comfortable. "When I was a child I saw a magazine at the careers' office advertising a course at the London College of Fashion," says Hare. "At the time we considered fashion to be Sergio Tacchini tracksuits. I thought: 'What do they teach there, how to make tracksuits?' When I see an ethnic kid say, "Fuck it, I'm going to get an education, I'm going to compete,' it always brings a tear to my eye. To fight within the system is braver than to stand outside it being a bad boy."

NIGEL
CABOURN

FOUNDER

The world of menswear is full of obsessives, always has been. In the Sixties they were driven by the Modern Jazz Quartet and mohair, in the Seventies by T-shirt provenance, in the Eighties by imported denim, and ever since the Nineties by… well, everything. Hipster lore is self-determining, and if you venture north of Columbia Road on a Sunday morning and stroll up to the bookshops in Broadway Market you'll pass dozens of bearded men in pinched tweed, men whose looks didn't just happen by accident, didn't just sprout from an Oxfam shop. Modern obsessives care about everything from the sizing of belt loops to the height of a turn-up, from the sheen on a pocket square to the hole punches on a pair of brogues. Casualwear is these days is no different from formally tailored clothing, and the attention to detail and fabrication is often as luxurious as it is in bespoke tailoring. Men are drawn to heritage brands and legacy products because fashion moves too fast; plaid shirts, depth, difficult banjo music. Something grown up and studied. This is why Nigel Cabourn is having such a renaissance. Professionally he has been around since the Eighties, when he accidentally built a cult following in Japan and was spoken of in hushed tones in Shoreditch and Dalston. Yet his moment is right now, right this minute. His collections have always been influenced by military uniforms and vintage clothing, using fabrics such as Harris tweed, gabardine, and Ventile—a material developed by the Shirley Institute in the late Thirties for aircraftmen flying across the North Sea. If they were shot down, it kept them afloat and warm.

OLIVER SPENCER

FOUNDER

It would be difficult to find anyone to say a bad word about Oliver Spencer. Actually, not difficult—impossible. One of the fundamental differences between the menswear industry and the womenswear industry is the former's collegiate atmosphere, particularly in London, and designers are more than happy to help each other out. Spencer is certainly like this, but then he himself has asked for help in the past. After he'd established himself with the tailoring venture Favourbrook (his waistcoats famously appeared in *Four Weddings and a Funeral*), having launched his own label he went looking for sponsorship. The first person he approached was Topman's design director, Gordon Richardson. Richardson's response was suitably straightforward. "He said, 'We couldn't sponsor an established designer like you but just do a bloody show and you won't believe what happens,'" explains Spencer. "So we did, in an old banana warehouse in Covent Garden. It was like someone had turned the lights on." As *GQ*'s Robert Johnston says, "The aesthetic may be different, but Spencer's take on fashion has a similar appeal to Paul Smith's—providing clothes that are never scary but always cool to men who want to stand out from the crowd without shouting about it. Pretty much perfect, in fact." Spencer has made a virtue of including celebrities and bold-face names in his shows at London Collections: Men, proving his influence as well as his growing stature in the industry.

SIR
PAUL SMITH

FOUNDER

Paul Smith, CBE, is the godfather of British menswear, the man who, in the Eighties, brought a completely new sensibility to men's retailing by fusing the traditional and the quirky; he deemed this new idea "classic with a twist" and never looked back. Journalist Paul Morley wrote that David Bowie was "the human equivalent of a Google search," and in a way you could say the same thing about Paul Smith. Walk into his Covent Garden office and you'll find yourself entering an extraordinary Aladdin' cave of the arcane, the eccentric, and the ridiculously modish. This is where Smith comes to do his thinking, though how he can keep his mind on the matter in hand is mystifying because his inner sanctum is a hodge-podge of cultural tidbits, a cornucopia of the cool and the absurd. "The office is the equivalent of my brain," he says. There are piles of everything from clockwork robots and water pistols to old copies of *Vogue*, *Nova*, and *Town*; tatty cardboard boxes filled with antique cameras and painted shirts, Victorian birthday cards and old maps of Paris; dustbin bags full of toy rabbits, plastic watches, rubber fish, and enamel lapel pins from British holiday resorts which have long since faded from memory. There are also several prototypes sent by his friend Jonathan Ive (Smith is often the first person in the country to see the latest iteration of Ive's phones, tablets and watches). In the best possible sense Paul Smith has always been a sponge, and his attitude toward his work exemplifies this. He is still a bastion of Great British Design (cap. G, cap. B, cap. D), yet has also become one of our greatest design ambassadors. And, seemingly, he is a man who never stops.

PRIVATE WHITE V.C.

NICK ASHLEY, CREATIVE DIRECTOR

A true military hero and founding father of the Manchester factory that now manufactures clothing in his name, Jack White was born in Leeds in 1896. He was awarded the Victoria Cross during the First World War, and on returning home, embarked upon an apprenticeship as a trainee pattern cutter at the local factory, rising through the ranks to become general manager and then owner. During his time as owner, White laid the foundations of what the factory is today, bringing with him Yorkshire influences which led to the company specialising in woollen garments, rather than just the traditional Lancashire cotton raincoats and mackintoshes. In 1997, the company was acquired by Jack White's great grandchildren. The new clothing line gives a subtle nod to White's military legacy, with many items based on classic wartime pieces, updated with added functionality and detail for the modern man. Materials are sourced locally, while the collection is designed by Nick Ashley, Private White V. C.'s creative director. Ashley has a long and illustrious history in the fashion industry, having worked for Kenzo, Tod's, and Dunhill among others. For some time he also had his own brand of luxury motorcycle clothing and produced ome of the finest fleeces ever made. "Private White V. C. is a high integrity brand," he has said. "Starting with wool on a sheep, weaving it locally, carefully constructing the clothes in Manchester and selling them with love to people who care about such things. These clothes are for people who have an emotional attachment to the clothes that accompany them through life."

RICHARD JAMES

SEAN DIXON, CO-FOUNDER
&
TOBY LAMB, DESIGN AND BRAND DIRECTOR

Even after three decades, Richard James is still considered by many to be the new boy in Savile Row. This persists, even though the boy is now a brand, even though it has two stores—bespoke and off-the-peg—and even though it is almost a British institution. They were once known for colour-blocked ties and skinny two-piece suits with slash pockets and crazy linings, as well as for fabrics—tartans, denim, AstroTurf, the lot. A Richard James suit was the kind you could spot from fifty paces, and in some cases could see from space. They were modernist, they were gothic, they were extravagant—and they told anyone who saw you wearing one that you really cared about the way you looked. These days the brand is different, broader, quieter in some respects, but at the same time bigger, more ambitious. Keen to be involved. Menswear brands nowadays can't afford not to cover all the bases, and because the customer base is so much bigger, the offer needs to cater to it. While it is never a good idea to be all things to all men, there is also a sense that men still want a one-stop-shop. Which is why you'll find the likes of Richard James offering everything from ready-to-wear suits, outerwear, knitwear and accessories, from cufflinks to gloves. The brand is now run by managing director Sean Dixon, who started the brand with Richard James back when God was a boy—and when Savile Row was a very different place indeed.

SEAN SUEN

FOUNDER

Sean Suen was educated as a painter, practiced as a graphic designer, and is now founder and head designer of Chinese streetwear label Sean Suen, which launched in Beijing in 2012. Suen's ethos follows the core principle of remaining amusing, dynamic, and chic, and merges punk-rock influences, such as aggressive metallics, piercings, and tattoos, with urban streetwear and Chinese elegance. Suen's designs feature loose, fluid silhouettes in contrasting hefty fabrics, reflecting his wish to combine the "masculinity and structure of the European suit" with "the elegance of the Chinese robe." Suen's spring/summer 2016 collection revolved around silk robes as well as black-and-white pinstriped smocks and suits resembling optical illusions. The collection aimed to weld Suen's Chinese heritage with the comparatively alien West, and Suen used his personal travel diary, which charts his journey from China to London., as inspiration The collection was also inspired by Chinese chess. "It's not only about two sides against each other," says Suen. "It's also about the communication between you and your opponent, history, reality, cultures of East and West."

SIBLING

SID BRYAN, COZETTE MCCREERY, CO-FOUNDERS

One of London's most creative design teams was launched in 2007, when Sid Bryan, Joe Bates, and Cozette McCreery were on holiday in Ibiza. They scanned the recent menswear shows online, saw only a sea of grey, and decided to do something about that. They launched a raggle-taggle collection at a party the following year; but even though a team of Japanese retail buyers were politely queuing up to buy it, nothing was for sale. Critical success forced them into commercial production, and ever since their collections have become stronger and stronger, while their shows are a regular highlight of London Collections: Men. Their designs have become tabloid fodder for those newspapers that don't really understand the purpose of fashion, and yet they occupy a space similar to the one vacated by BodyMap back in the Eighties; they nod slightly to the wonderful world of Leigh Bowery, and smile as they do so. Their shows have included everything from bottom-baring US football pants and pink pom-pom balaclavas, to collaborations with Woolmark and tailor Edward Sexton, and all are rather wonderful. As for their customers, "It's not a camp, carefree eccentric," says Bryan. "Most of our customers are normal blokes. Quite a few of our guys are in film production, graphic design, the music industry." Even David Beckham buys Sibling, although it's not known where. The team are now a duo, as Joe Bates lost his battle with cancer in 2015.

THOM SWEENEY

TOM WHIDDETT & LUKE SWEENEY, FOUNDERS

When designers try to reinvent the retail experience, they usually do so by conjuring up grand visions fashioned from steel, glass, and acres of impossibly brutalist reinforced white Perspex. In fact there is still a sense that a modern shopping environment has to look like the box your latest Apple product came in. A big white box, mind, but a white box all the same. London, however, is predictably different in this respect, and as it is full of genuinely traditional men's outfitters, there is now a new generation of designers who have no qualms about making their shops look as though they were first opened in the late–nineteenth or early–twentieth century. Take the Thom Sweeney store in Weighhouse Street in Mayfair. This little piece of London's most obviously upmarket shopping district—nicknamed North Mayfair—is "coming up," as estate agents still like to say. Here you have Jeremy King and Chris Corbin's Beaumont hotel, you have the shops in Duke Street, and you have a host of new little restaurants that are forcing people to stroll north of Grosvenor Square. And of course you have Thom Sweeney's beautiful townhouse, a bespoke tailor shop that feels as though it has been transported direct from Victorian London via Miami circa 1930, Los Angeles circa 1940, and possibly New York circa 1965. *GQ* christened it an "immersive man-temple, a man-lair of note." It is chic, as are the men who own it. Luke Sweeney and Thom Whiddett used to work for master tailor Timothy Everest, and in addition to creating beautiful shopping environments, they also produce beautiful bespoke suits—significantly sharply-cut three-pieces complete with horseshoe waistcoats, grey flannel two-pieces, hopsack blazers, and brushed-cotton chinos. You could call these clothes new duds with an old-fashioned sensibility, or old duds with a newfound sensibility. Either way, they work.

TIGER OF SWEDEN

ANDREAS GRAN, CREATIVE DIRECTOR

It speaks volumes that TOS decided that London was the perfect place to showcase their collections, as it underscores yet again that London is a platform for international designers as well as domestic ones, no matter how big or how small. One of the reasons they decided to show here is because of the diverse nature of the city's designers, assuming — quite rightly — that their Scandinavian aesthetic — an austere simplicity — would play well. They have made their name by designing razor-sharp suits, excelling at the kind of tailoring that many brands talk about, but don't always deliver. The brand is also beholden to "the twist", as their spring/summer 2017 collection showed. In the wake of various waves of extreme nationalism spreading across Europe, and in anticipation of the British European referendum, the show offered a multi-cultural theme, a collection of huge diversity on many different levels. The show was full of references to melding, and emphasized the importance of political as well as sartorial shape-shifting. Here it all was, cutting-edge and classic, streetwear and suiting, pattern and solidity. Their mission statement says it all: go on their website and you'll be treated with the following — "Tiger of Sweden was established in 1903. Then redefined in 1993. Now we are evolving."

TOM FORD

FOUNDER

"Everyone in Tom Ford's office looks beautiful. Those who aren't physically beautiful at least look beautiful in their perfectly tailored Tom Ford suits and dresses," the comedian David Walliams observed when he went to interview Ford for *GQ* a while back. "Ford's room exudes sex and power, the two main themes of his work.," Walliams continued. "There are erotic advertising campaign photographs on the walls, a huge, dark wooden desk, an impossibly high ceiling." And, of course, there's Tom Ford. The designer always looks immaculate, and he always looks as though he has just stepped out of one of his own campaigns, probably wearing stubble, a white shirt, and a black suit. Ford's decision to move his presentation from Milan to London for London Collections: Men was, like the decision to do the same by Burberry and Alexander McQueen, one of the reasons the event took off so quickly, and his support for London—where he mostly lives—and for British menswear in particular, has been comprehensive, fulsome, and genuine. He has always been something of an anglophile, which he displayed with panache when he took over from Brioni as James Bond's tailor of choice after *Casino Royale*. In *Quantum of Solace*, *Skyfall*, and *Spectre* he has managed to make the world's most famous spy even cooler, at least sartorially, by dressing him in tab-collar shirts, shawl-collared blue evening jackets, off-white evening dress, charcoal three-piece suits, and the like. "I am actually extremely casual in certain environments," he has said. "But one of the reasons I like living in London, I like the formality of it, as compared to the formality of America—or informality. I like putting on a suit. I like putting on a tie."

TOMMY HILFIGER

FOUNDER

London loves Tommy and Tommy loves London. Having been one of the most influential American fashion designers of his generation, it made sense to solicit help from Hilfiger when we were launching London Collections: Men. Every season since the launch in 2012, he has had a presence at LCM, throwing parties, hosting dinners, showing his collections, and acting as an international ambassador. For thirty years, Hilfiger has brought "classic American cool" apparel to consumers around the world. His designs give time-honoured classics a fresh look, and his discerning taste has provided the foundation for the growth of a global brand. Under Hilfiger's guidance, vision and leadership as principal designer, the Tommy Hilfiger Group has become one of very few globally-recognized designer brands offering a wide range of American-inspired apparel and accessories. However he is a surprisingly humble man, something that came to the fore when he decided to launch his brand, back in 1985. Having approached the advertising guru George Lois, he was initially uncomfortable with the campaign suggestion. The ad that Lois came up with depicted a fill-in-the-blank style list with the names of the world's most popular clothing designers—including Ralph Lauren, Perry Ellis, and Calvin Klein—suggesting that Hilfiger should be added to the list. hilfiger was mortified. These people were legends to him, and as a relative newcomer, he didn't feel qualified to be listed among their ranks. None-the-less, Lois convinced Hilfiger to run the campaign, which included a billboard in Times Square. It worked.

While Philip Green's brand was founded as long ago as 1978, it is only in the last fifteen years that it has become synonymous with cutting-edge high street fashion. Before Topman reinvented it, the British high street was infamous for taking designer product and fast-tracking bastardised copies, infuriating designers, and bringing the cheaper end of the business into disrepute. Topman injected some much-needed cool into the high street, as well as some genuine fashion innovation. The creative powerhouse behind the brand is Gordon Richardson, who has been with Topman since 2000, and was made creative director in 2012. "Menswear is in the healthiest state I've ever witnessed in my career," he said in 2015. "With the MAN show and London Collections: Men inspiring other cities such as New York to follow suit, it feels like at last menswear is getting the recognition it deserves."

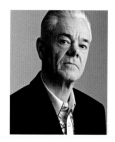

TOPMAN

GORDON RICHARDSON, CREATIVE DIRECTOR

VIVIENNE
WESTWOOD

FOUNDER

It is impossible to overstate just how important Vivienne Westwood is in the narrative of modern British menswear. If she had stopped producing clothes in 1978, she would still be remembered as one of the greatest designers of the twentieth century. Certainly she is the most important architect of fashion insurrection there has ever been. Not only was she largely responsible for most of the tropes of the punk archetype—tartan, bondage strides, leather, straps, spikes—but she then reinvented herself as a catwalk goliath, pushing the culture where it didn't know it was meant to go. Along with her former partner Malcolm McLaren, she remains a dominant and often inscrutable crucible for British youth culture. There has been a tendency recently to take her for granted, yet her flair, her design touch, and her refusal to engage with the establishment makes everything she does worth recognising, worth celebrating. "I do things that irritate people," she says. "I'm always saving things, telling people to turn taps off. The world's forgotten more than it knows. Consumption is about throwing away the past. But to engage with the world we must engage with the past through art and reading. It gives you a critique of your own life, and you realise: 'I'm not doing anything. Human beings are capable of amazing things and I'm just sucking things up.'"

XANDER ZHOU

FOUNDER

One of the principle aims of London Collections: Men has been to act as a platform for global menswear, not just home-grown designers, so it is an actual delight when designers from abroad decide to show here every January and June. Dozens of international brands have had a profile in London during LCM, including Moschino, Tod's, Dolce & Gabbana, Coach, Tommy Hilfiger, Tiger Of Sweden, Tom Ford, CMMN SWDN, Rag & Bone, Song Zio, Wan Hung, Soulland, Angelo Galasso, and Joseph Abboud. One Chinese designer who has made LCM his home is Xander Zhou. After studying fashion in the Netherlands, he established his label and studio in Beijing, where he quickly made a name for himself as a menswear designer. In his designs, Zhou likes to explore the boundaries between form and function, as well as the unique qualities of the different fabrics he uses. He reconstructs classical forms by providing them with new contexts, occasionally blurring gender stereotypes in the process. His collections are usually inspired by youth subcultures, and combine simple elegance with a streetwise attitude. He was particularly responsive when David Bowie died, offering craftily realised homages to the singer himself. Exploring thirteen themes—including diversity, gender identity, freedom, fetish, inclusiveness and emancipation (to quote *Wonderland* magazine)—Zhou made the catwalk sing.

YMC

FRASER MOSS, FOUNDER

You Must Create was formed in London in 1995 by Fraser Moss and Jimmy Collins in response to increasing demand for stylish, functional, modern menswear. Their design ethos is borrowed from the pioneer of American industrial design Raymond Loewy, who, when asked how he saw the future of design, said emphatically: "You must create your own design-style." It is this philosophy that has inspired YMC since it started. Ignoring current trends, they build their collections season upon season, always trying to stay true to the brand's origins. Timeless is the word that best describes the clothing, but a timeless spirit is hard to capture in the modern world of menswear, which demands a furious turnover. YMC's shows at London Collections: Men are as distinctive as their clothes, and just as forthright. Who else would design an indigo brocade collarless jacket?

FASHION DIRECTORY

ABOUT TOWN

LONDON MENSWEAR SHOPPING

PRIVATE WHYTE V.C.

The Garbstore
118 Kensington Park Road,
Portobello, W11 2ES
couvertureandthegarbstore.com

LN-CC
Late Night Chameleon Café,
18 Shacklewell Lane, Dalston, E8 2EZ
ln-cc.com

Present
140 Shoreditch High Street, E1 6JE
present-london.com

The Goodhood Store
151 Curtain Road, EC2A 3QE
goodhoodstore.com

Hub
2A Ada Street, Broadway Market,
E8 4QU
hubshop.co.uk

Liberty
Regent Street, W1B 5AH
libertylondon.com

Hostem
28 Old Nichol Street, E2 7HR
hostem.co.uk

Matches
87 Marylebone High Street,
W1U 4QU
matchesfashion.com/mens

Selfridges
Oxford Street, W1
selfridges.com/menswear

Opening Ceremony
35 King Street, Covent Garden,
WC2E 8JG
openingceremony.us

Harrods
87-135 Brompton Road, Knightsbridge,
SW1X 7XL
harrods.com/men

Stuarts London
35-37 Uxbridge Road, W12 8LH
stuartslondon.com

Wolf & Badger
46 Ledbury Road, Notting Hill, W11
wolfandbadger.com

Trunk Clothiers
8 Chiltern Street, W1U 7PU
trunkclothiers.com

The Other Shop
21 Kingly Street, W1B 5QA
other-shop.com

Topman General Store
98 Commercial Street, E1 6LZ
topman.com

Dover Street Market
Haymarket, W1
doverstreetmarket.com

Harvey Nichols
109-125 Knightsbridge, SW1X 7RJ
harveynichols.com/mens

The Shop at Bluebird
350 King's Road, SW3
theshopatbluebird.com

Browns
23-27 South Molton Street, W1
brownsfashion.com

Duke Street Emporium
55 Duke Street, W1K
dukestreetemporium.com

Oi Polloi
1 Marshall Street, W1F 9BA
oipolloi.com

E TAUTZ

The Vintage Showroom
14 Earlham Street, Covent Garden WC2
thevintageshowroom.com

Crazy Man Crazy
18 Church Road, SE19 2ET
crazymancrazylondon.co.uk

The Content Store
28 Lambs Conduit Street, WC1N 3LE
contentstorelondon.com

Sefton
196 Upper Street, N1 1RQ
seftonfashion.com

HUH store
56 Stoke Newington Road N16 7XB
store.huhmagazine.co.uk

Layers
39 S Molton Street, W1K 5RN
layerslondon.com

Sneakerstuff
107-108 Shoreditch High Street, E1 6JN
sneakersnstuff.com

Number Six
The Old Truman Brewery,
6 Dray Walk, E1 6QL
numbersixlondon.com

Machine A
13 Brewer Street, W1F 0RH
machine-a.com

Primitive
73-75 Shacklewell Lane, E8 2EB
shop.primitivelondon.co.uk

Cad and the Dandy
13 Savile Row, W1S 3NE
cadandthedandy.co.uk

Thom Sweeney
1-2 Weighhouse Street, W1K 5LR
thomsweeney.co.uk

YMC
D'Arblay House, 11 Poland Street,
W1F 8QA
youmustcreate.com

Oliver Spencer
62 Lambs Conduit Street, WC1N 3LW
oliverspencer.co.uk

E.Tautz
71 Duke Street, W1K 5NX
etautz.com

Son of a Stag
9 Dray Walk, E1 6QL
sonofastag.com

Richard James
29 Savile Row, W1
richardjames.co.uk

B store
24A Savile Row, W1S 3PR,

Gieves & Hawkes
1 Savile Row, W1S 3JR
gievesandhawkes.com

Albam
23 Beak Street, W1F 9RS
albamclothing.com

Emma Willis
66 Jermyn Street, SW1Y 6NY
emmawillis.com

Private Whyte V.C.
73 Duke Street, W1K 5NR
privatewhitevc.com

A Child of the Jago
10 Great Eastern Street,
EC2A 3NT
achildofthejago.com

Oki Ni *oki-ni.com/en/latest*

Farfetch *farfetch.com*

Cover photograph © Daniel Riera

London map © London's Kerning Poster; nbstudio.co.uk

p. 4: Advertisement for Terylene, Richard Orme, Tony Newton and Peter Christian, 27 January 1960, London, Photograph Terence Donovan © Terence Donovan Archive

p. 5: Songzio show during The London Collections Men SS17 at the BFC Show on June 10, 2016 in London © Tristan Fewings/ Stringer/Getty

p. 6: Carnaby Street, London, 1960s © Topfoto.co.uk

p. 6: (bottom) Wall Sign, Carnaby Street W1, London, 1997 © Patrick Barth/REX/Shutterstock

p. 7: Bowler hat © Shutterstock

p. 8: Andrew Jarman, London, 2016 © Jonathan Daniel Pryce

p. 9: The Ivy Shop Logo © John Simons Apparel Company

p. 11: John Stephen, a tailor in Carnaby Street, London, 1964 © Keystone Features/Stringer/Getty

p. 11: John Stephen Clothes Shop, Carnaby Street, London, 1967 © Donald Brooks/Rex/Shutterstock

p. 14: Trojan and Mark Vaultier, London, 1986 © Derek Ridgers

p. 15: Jim, a punk in Streatham, South London, 1976 © Janette Beckman/Getty

p. 16–17: Tommy Hilfiger, Dee Ocleppo and Prince Charles, London Collections: Men launch reception, St James's Palace, London © Richard Young/REX/Shutterstock

p. 20: Hu Bing, LCM ambassador at the Dunhill cocktail event, June 2016, London © Darren Gerrish

p. 20: Lulu Kennedy, London, 2013 © Toni & Guy Haircare Products

p. 20: Tinie Tempah and Lewis Hamilton at the LCM Opening Reception, June 2015, London © Darren Gerrish

p. 20: David Bowie, Interview magazine, Los Angeles, California, 1994 © Michel Haddi/Contour by Getty

p. 20: Dylan Jones and the LCM ambassadors at the Opening Event, January, 2015, London © Nigel Pacquette

p. 20: Tommy Hilfiger and Dylan Jones celebrate London Collections Men AW16 at Mortons in London, 2016 © James Mason

p. 24: Hu Bing, 2015 © Simon Webb

p. 25: Sean Frank, 2014 © Rhys Frampton

p. 26: Manrutt Wongkaew, 2015 © Simon Webb

p. 27: Adio Marchant, Bipolar Sunshine, 2014 © Rhys Frampton

p. 28: Samm Henshaw, 2016 © Simon Webb

p. 29: Jack Guinness, 2014 © Mike Blackett

p. 30: Jim Chapman, 2014 © Mike Blackett

p. 31: Bayode Oduwole, 2014 © Mike Blackett

p. 32: Aman Singh, 2015 © Mike Blackett

p. 33: James Bay, 2015 © Simon Webb

p. 34: Jason Atherton, 2015 © Simon Webb

p. 35: Jonathan Daniel Pryce, 2016 © Simon Webb

p. 36: Tony Ward, 2014 © Mike Blackett

p. 37: James Nuttal, 2014 © Mike Blackett

p. 38–39: Martell Campbell, London, 2014 © Jonathan Daniel Pryce; ©Shutterstock

p. 40: Charlie, London, 2015 © Jonathan Daniel Pryce

p. 41: Magnus Ronning, London, 2016 © Jonathan Daniel Pryce

p. 42: Laurie Belgrave, London, 2014 © Jonathan Daniel Pryce

p. 43: Giulio Aprin, London, 2014 © Jonathan Daniel Pryce

p. 44: London, 2016 © Jonathan Daniel Pryce

p. 45: London, 2016 © Jonathan Daniel Pryce

p. 46: London, 2016 © Jonathan Daniel Pryce

p. 47: William Gilchrist, London, 2015 © Jonathan Daniel Pryce

p. 48: Matt Hambly, London, 2016 © Jonathan Daniel Pryce

p. 49: Kings Way, London, 2016 © Jonathan Daniel Pryce

p. 50–51: Gregory Farmer, Creative Director at Brutus, London, 2014 © Jonathan Daniel Pryce © Shutterstock

p. 52: Gordon Richardson, Topman, 2014 © Jonathan Daniel Pryce

p. 53: Michael Dave, London, 2014 © Jonathan Daniel Pryce

p. 54: Kieron Watts, London, 2014 © Jonathan Daniel Pryce

p. 55: Harry J Irving, London, 2014 © Jonathan Daniel Pryce

p. 56: Christopher Millington, London, 2014 © Jonathan Daniel Pryce

p. 57: Serge Rigvava, London, 2016 © Jonathan Daniel Pryce

p. 58: Kadu Dantas, London, 2015 © Jonathan Daniel Pryce

p. 59: Timur, London, 2015 © Jonathan Daniel Pryce

p. 60–61: GQ Style AW14 © Photography Rebecca Thomas; Styling Victoria Higgs; © Shutterstock

p. 62–63: GQ Style AW14 © Photography Rebecca Thomas; Styling Victoria Higgs

p. 64–65: GQ Style AW14 © Rebecca Thomas; Styling Victoria Higgs

p. 66–67: GQ Style AW14 © Rebecca Thomas; Styling Victoria Higgs

p. 68–69: GQ Style AW14 © Mark Kean; Styling Gary Armstrong

p. 70–71: Hugo Kreit, 2015 © Jonathan Daniel Pryce © Shutterstock

p. 72: Oliver Greenall, London, 2015 © Jonathan Daniel Pryce

p. 73: Harry James Irving, London, 2013 © Jonathan Daniel Pryce

p. 74: Kadu Dantas, Victoria House, 2015 © Jonathan Daniel Pryce

p.   75: Grant Pearce, London, 2016 © Jonathan Daniel Pryce

p.   76: KK Obi, London, 2014 © Jonathan Daniel Pryce

p.   77: London, 2015 © Jonathan Daniel Pryce

p.   78: Johnson Gold, London, 2014 © Jonathan Daniel Pryce

p.   79: David Gandy, London, 2016 © Jonathan Daniel Pryce

p.   80: London, 2016 © Jonathan Daniel Pryce

p.   81: Old Sorting Office, London, 2014 © Jonathan Daniel Pryce

p.   82: Eshan Kali and John Jarrett, LCM, 2016
      © Jonathan Daniel Pryce

p.   83: Marcus Jaye and Chris Benns, London, 2014
      © Jonathan Daniel Pryce

p.   84–93: Pinstripe Punks, GQ Style AW14
      © Thomas Cooksey; Styling Luke Day; © Shutterstock

p.   95–103: Like A Rolling Stone, GQ Style AW14 © Sean Thomas;
      Styling Jo Levin; Stylist's assistant Holly Roberts; Production
      Grace Gilfeather © Shutterstock

p.   104–115: West End Boys, GQ 2014 © Dylan Don; Styling
      Jo Levin © Shutterstock. Models: George and Max Tree at
      Select, Eli and Harrison at Elite, Levi and Matthew at Next,
      James Hampson and Stas at FM.

p.   116–125: Taking Care of Business, GQ 2016 © Daniel Riera;
      Styling Luke Day; © Shutterstock

p.   126–135: Brit Pop, GQ Style AW14 © Scott Trindle;
      Styling Luke Day

p.   138–139: © Nigel Pacquette © Agi & Sam Catwalking

p.   140–141: © Hazel Gaskin © Courtesy of Alexander McQueen
      © Trunk Xu

p.   142–143: © Hans Zeuthen © Ashley Verse © Astrid Anderson

p.   144–145: © Baartmans & Siegel
      © Amber Siegel/Wouter Baartmans

p.   146–147: © Belstaff

p.   148–149: © Burberry © Ashley Verse © Joshua Lawrence

p.   150–151: © Katinka Herbert © Chris Moore © Ashley Verse
      © Casely-Hayford

p.   152–153: © Rory Payne © Christopher Kane

p.   154–155: © Joshua Lawrence © Sam Scott-Hunter
      © Christopher Raeburn

p.   156–157: © Nicholas Kay © Christopher Shannon

p.   158–159: © Coach

p.   160–161: © Hazel Gaskin © Craig Green

p.   162–163: © Stefano Babic © Dolce & Gabbana
      © Jason Lloyd-Evans

p.   164–165: © Rankin © Dsquared2

p.   166–167: © Courtesy of Alfred Dunhill © Andrew Vowles

p.   168–169: © Rhys Frampton © Ashley Verse © E. Tautz

p.   170–171: © Nigel Pacquette © Gives & Hawkes

p.   172–173: © Hackett London

p.   174–175: © Mike Blackett © Beccy Nuthall for Toni & Guy
      © Jeff Spicer/Getty © Hardy Amies

p.   176–177: © James Long

p.   178–179: © J.W.Anderson

p.   180–181: © Duo Blau © Katie Eary

p.   182–183: © Kent & Curwen

p.   184–185: © Courtesy of Nick Knight Studio © Kilgour

p.   186–187: © Patrick Cox © Rebecca Maynes © Lathbridge

p.   188–189: © Lee Roach Studio

p.   190–191: © Liam Hodges © Ellis Scott

p.   192–193: © Lou Dalton

p.   194–195: © Maharishi

p.   196–197: © Margaret Howell © Joshua Lawrence
      © Jill Kennington

p.   198–199: © Matthew Miller

p.   200–201: © Ashley Verse © Joshua Lawrence © Moschino
      © Giampaolo Sgura

p.   202–203: © Marc Hare-Mr Hare © Nikolas Ventourakis
      © Sam Wilson © Shaun James Cox

p.   204–205: © Ben Benoliel © Nigel Cabourn

p.   206–207: © Hazel Gaskin © Oliver Spencer

p.   208–209: © Paul Smith

p.   210–211: © Hazel Gaskin © Private White V.C

p.   212–213: © Richard James

p.   214–215: © Sean Suen © Ashley Verse

p.   216–217: © Ashley Verse © NOWfashion © Matt Irwin
      © Sibling

p.   218–219: © Thom Sweeney

p.   220–221: © Tiger Of Sweden ©Ashley Verse

p.   222–223: Tom Ford Portrait © Simon Perry © Tom Ford

p.   224–225: © Ashley Verse © Tommy Hilfiger
      © Darren Gerrish

p.   226–227: © Hazel Gaskin © Jason Lloyd Evans © Scott Trindle
      © Topman

p.   228–229: © Paolo Colaiocco © Sudhir Pithwa
      © Vivienne Westwood

p.   230–231: © Xander Zhou

p.   232–233: © YMC

p.   234–235: © London's Kerning Poster; nbstudio.co.uk ©Alamy

p.   236–237: © E. Tautz © Private White V.C.

p.   240: © Nicholas Kay

      Back cover © Rebecca Thomas

First and foremost I would like to thank Paul Solomons for designing such a beautiful book; this book is as much his as it is mine. Thanks also to the wonderful Jacob Lehman for commissioning the book, Tracey Emin for suggesting it in the first place, and the marvelous Jonathan Daniel Pryce for taking so many of the photographs.

Thanks also to Jonathan Newhouse, Nicholas Coleridge, Sarah Walter, Edie Walter Jones, Georgia Sydney Jones, Ed Victor, Natalie Massenet, Caroline Rush, Jane Boardman, David Hicks, Anna Akopyan, Cai Lunn, Simon Webb, Luke Day, Mark Russell, Rhys Frampton, Mike Blackett, Dylan Don, Thomas Cooksey, Daniel Riera, Scott Trindle, Sean Thomas, Rebecca Thomas, Mark Kean, Jo Levin, Victoria Higgs, Gary Armstrong, Lottie Stanners, Eleanor Halls and Grace Gilfeather.

I would also like to thank all the London Collections Men (or London Fashion Week Men's as it soon became known) designers, because without you, this book wouldn't have a reason to exist. It is you who have made London menswear so exciting, you who have attracted the world's media to the capital, you who are a testament to our innate design talent. Thank you.

Dylan Jones has written twenty books on subjects as diverse as music and politics and fashion and photography. His book about the Conservative Leader David Cameron, *Cameron On Cameron*, was shortlisted for the Channel Four Political Book Of The Year, while his biography of Jim Morrison, *Dark Star*, was a *New York Times* best seller. He has been an editor at *The Observer*, *The Sunday Times*, *i-D*, *The Face* and *Arena*, and is currently the Editor-In-Chief of *GQ*. He is a trustee of the Hay Festival and a board member of the Norman Mailer Colony. He was awarded an OBE in the Queen's Honours List in 2013. He lives in London and Powys with his family.